Advance praise for *YOU'RE SO MONEY*

"Farnoosh Torabi's book is a hilarious must-read for anyone who wants to live like a king, even if he's just a lowly serf with nothing in his bank account but blighted turnips, and, like, $3,000."

—Ben Lerer, cofounder of Thrillist.com

P9-DCD-835

"Farnoosh knows so much about personal finance that I practically make more money just looking at her. And reading *You're So Money* gave me the advice I needed to keep my good life rolling."

—James Altucher, founder of Stockpickr.com

"In a clear and witty way, Farnoosh tells you from experience how to jump-start your money."

—Susan Beacham, founder of Money Savvy Generation

"After I read *You're So Money*, I immediately ordered copies to give to my three children in college. The lessons of the book define one of the best courses they could take. Indeed, this is a must-read for every college student—enjoyable, informative, and a powerful guide for the next phase of their lives and beyond."

—James B. Thomas, Dean, Smeal College of Business,
   The Pennsylvania State University

"Farnoosh Torabi's *You're So Money* is the perfect blend of fresh advice and bold attitude necessary to educate a horribly underserved generation about personal finance."

—Jim Cramer, host of CNBC's *Mad Money* and author of *Stay Mad for Life*

"*You're So Money* is the best financial book for young people I have read in ten years. Farnoosh's style is entertaining, straight to the point, and powerful. You'll laugh as you read and learn how fun it can be to live and finish rich!"

—David Bach, #1 *New York Times* bestselling author of
   The Automatic Millionaire and *Start Late, Finish Rich*

YOU'RE SO MONEY

YOU'RE SO

MONEY

LIVE RICH, EVEN WHEN YOU'RE NOT

Farnoosh Torabi

 THREE RIVERS PRESS • NEW YORK

Copyright © 2008 by Farnoosh Torabi
Foreword and "How Stock Speculating Can Make You Rich," copyright © 2008 by
James J. Cramer

All rights reserved.

Published in the United States by Three Rivers Press, an imprint of the Crown
Publishing Group, a division of Random House, Inc., New York.
www.crownpublishing.com

Three Rivers Press and the Tugboat design are registered trademarks of Random
House, Inc.

Library of Congress Cataloging-in-Publication Data
Torabi, Farnoosh.
    You're so money : live rich, even when you're not / Farnoosh Torabi; featuring a
foreword and investing tips by James J. Cramer.
        p.   cm.
    Includes index.
    1. Finance, Personal—Handbooks, manuals, etc.   2. Young adults—Finance,
Personal—Handbooks, manuals, etc.   I. Cramer, Jim.   II. Title.
    HG179.T67 2008
    332.024—dc22

                                                                    2007046715

ISBN 978-0-307-40619-4

Printed in the United States of America

Design by Ruth Lee-Mui

10 9 8 7 6 5 4 3 2 1

First Edition

For Mom, Dad, and Todd

Acknowledgments

➤ ➤ ➤ Writing a book and getting it published takes hard work, little sleep, and, in my case, sacrificing a bit of sight (all those months in front of a laptop screen—not easy on the eyes). But beyond that, and more important, finishing a book and getting it on the shelves require tremendous luck. My luck is in knowing generous and inspiring individuals who have, in their own ways, helped make this book a reality. First and foremost, I'm lucky for the unconditional love and support of my family. My mother and father teach me, by example, that there are no limits to what you can achieve in life. My younger brother, Todd, keeps me laughing and thinking on my feet.

I am beyond fortunate for my best friend Tim Dussinger. A girl couldn't ask for a more loving steady. Thank you to my close friends for their enthusiasm and honest advice: Kate Dailey, Ariel Gornizky, Bethany Baumbach, Dustin Newcombe, Kat Ricker, Kafi Drexel, Dan Listwa, Margie Fox, Brian Maloney, David Dapko, Richard Laermer, Annika Pergament, Michael O'Looney, and Susan Beacham. You are such positive influences in my life. Thank you.

I have the enormous fortune of working with the extraordinary team at thestreet.com. First, thank you to Jim Cramer, who's graced this book with his invaluable advice. I am forever grateful. Thank you to CEO Tom Clarke and editor in chief David Morrow, who've granted me great freedom at work. Huge thank yous to Sandy Brown, James Altucher, Aaron Task, and Kristin Bentz. I love working together. Thank you for your support and friendships. Thank you, as well, to Bill McCandless, the executive editor of multimedia, and my hardworking, creative team at thestreet.com TV.

My researcher, friend, and go-to guy Tim Chan is a blessing. You will find his awesome anecdotes and fantastic ideas woven into this book. I am also lucky for the writing assistance of the great Cliff Mason. I still owe you a very expensive bottle of liquor.

Thank you to my literary agent Jeremy Katz of Sanford J. Greenburger for his brilliant guidance and backing. Thanks for taking a chance on me! I look forward to the next writing adventure with you! I must also thank Daniel Jacobson. He "got" me, and that was so encouraging.

I'm so lucky for the phenomenal editorial, marketing, and production team at Crown/Three Rivers Press, including my editor Lindsay Orman (you rock!), Carrie Thornton, and John Mahaney.

Thanks to Nancy Pertschuk, who taught me how to write in the tenth grade; my outstanding business professors at Penn State, Tim Simin and Greg Pierce; and David Andelman, my first and best mentor in New York. Thanks to my editors at *AM New York*. And thank you to Jean Chatzky, my first "real world" boss and constant inspiration.

I hope you all like my book. ☺

Contents

Foreword

➤ ➤ ➤ You're either brilliant for picking up this book or just plain lucky. Let me guess, you're probably not too far removed from college, maybe you've just gotten your first (or second) job, and you're struggling. Maybe it's the first time you've managed your own money (possibly because it's the first time you've had money to manage), or maybe you know a thing or two about personal finance, but you're so swamped in debt that you don't know if you can ever justify a Friday night out again. Personal finance books aren't your thing, but you know you need help, and Farnoosh's book looked friendlier than some of those others on the shelf, so you picked it up.

Congrats. You've come to the right place.

Now, I know what you're probably thinking. Jim, you're a millionaire. You couldn't possibly know what I'm going through or how I'm feeling. Oh, but I do! And man, do I wish I'd been smart or lucky enough to have this book in my hands when I was just starting out. In 1977 (before most of you were even born), I earned my first paycheck, a measly $178.82. That was posttaxes, postovertime, post–one week of criminal news reporting at the *Tallahassee Democrat*. Life was actually good at that point, considering that months later I would be homeless. My apartment burglarized and checking account emptied, I was sleeping in the back of my beat-up Ford Fairmont with only the weight of my Sierra Designs denim coat to keep me warm. This was not where I had pictured myself.

I realized that although money wasn't everything in life, it did buy a lot of stuff. And I wanted much more of it than I had at that moment. Criminal news reporting probably wasn't ever going to make me a wealthy man. But I did have another passion that might give me a shot. I loved the stock market with all its mysterious ticker symbols and furious trades and the potential for huge fortunes to be made if you knew how to play it right. That, in particular, is something I remember feeling under my skin and in my heart as far back as the fourth grade. I remember scouring the business pages of the *Philadelphia Evening Bulletin*, searching for the dollar signs and patterns that drove stock prices higher.

So I did some soul-searching, as there wasn't much else to do in my Fairmont. I thought about what I ultimately wanted to achieve in my life: like a wife and kids, a nice home, a comfortable lifestyle, season tickets to the Eagles, a golden retriever, annual vacations to exotic islands, a rewarding career, and a big enough stash of cash so that I could retire with money to spare and would never have to sleep in my car again! It became clear to me that it was time to turn my passion for the stock market into lots and lots of money so I could get what I wanted out of life.

This is why Farnoosh's book is so invaluable and why I jumped on the opportunity to be involved with *You're So Money*. Farnoosh asks you to envision what makes you happy, what it is that you truly desire in life, and then tells you how to achieve it, even when your finances are limited. She offers candid advice on how to manage your money when you're just starting out and presents opportunities instead of ultimatums. And if you're smart, you'll listen to her because she knows what she's talking about. While I was living in my car as a young professional, Farnoosh found a way to buy her own apartment while earning less than $50,000 a year. In Manhattan. On the Upper West Side. Let me tell you, that's no small feat.

I'm so sure of Farnoosh that we hired her back in 2006 to be thestreet.com's first official video correspondent. Her real-life savvy, hard-nosed journalism skills and financial background make her an asset to our site, especially as it expands and turns mainstream. She's interviewed everyone from Mark Cuban, Martha Stewart, and big-time CEOs to small business owners, NYSE floor traders, and investment gurus (including me. She interviews me daily on thestreet.com TV's *Wall Street Confidential*). Her style is inviting and engaging—not easy when you're discussing finance.

So take heart, whether you're reading this in your bedroom at Mom and Dad's, in the back of your beat-up Pontiac Grand Am, or in your snazzy new apartment that was just $100 more a month than you thought you could afford to spend, *You're So Money* can help you take control of your finances, which means not only getting more of the material things you want, but also enjoying the good life afforded by financial independence. People say "youth is wasted on the young." Prove them wrong. There's hope for you yet.

—James J. Cramer

YOU'RE SO MONEY

Introduction

➤ ➤ ➤ Perfect people can be so annoying. Like that zero-percent-body-fat girl who always beats you to yoga on Sunday mornings, wearing her perfect little Lululemon outfit. Once you saw her exit Starbucks carrying her usual $4 soy latte in one hand, a green leather Prada wallet in the other. You nearly cried (and by *you*, I mean me).

Perfect also works two cubicles away from you at the sausage mill, er work. He's the boyishly handsome recent hire who drives a new Audi and, rumor has it, plays golf with the boss. Lunch is usually fresh sushi. And his first-generation iPhone scores him "babes."

Who *are* these alien people, I ask, people whose lives seem so together that it physically pains us to acknowledge them? Two words, I suppose: *trust* and *fund*. Or, maybe it's *Beverly* and *Hills*? *Gold* and *digger*?

But, as my old Penn State roommate Amy Miller has taught me (and as I hope to illustrate in this book), having it all doesn't mean being superrich or even rich. It mostly means knowing what you want and what you absolutely *can't* live without, and then going for it.

A closer look at Amy: By day, she powers ten to twelve hours at a top Philadelphia law firm as a paralegal. By night, it's another three hours learning about tortes and intellectual property at Drexel law school. She envisions her life in ten years making well into six figures as a high-powered attorney with the occasional *Court TV* guest appearance. She'll summer by the lake in Maine and her Philadelphia penthouse will boast river views. It will also have one of those silent washing machines. She hasn't decided on the marriage thing.

Currently Amy's modest $42,000 a year salary is keeping her dreams at bay, but in the meantime, she's still managing to live it up. Even on her relatively small salary, she's able to stash away some money for retirement and to dabble in the stock market with stakes in Google and Toyota. She makes monthly payments toward her Stafford loan and always pays her $725 rent on the fifteenth. She also owns two pairs of Jimmy Choos and bought a very generous dinette set for her cousin who got married on a hilltop in Israel. Amy flew there first class.

Amy eats, too. Her favorite restaurant is Buddakan. And she's a Whole Foods fiend.

Hate her, right? But we really can't because Amy (and arguably Yoga Jenny and Sushi Sam) is doing all of this independently, sans mommy, daddy, or *sugar* daddy. My awesome friend is, instead, single-handedly experiencing "financial freedom" (gasp!), and believe you me it is by no means measured by the size of her paycheck or the $10,000 credit limit on her Visa. After taxes, Social Security, health care, and employee-sponsored retirement savings (we'll get to this later), Amy physically takes home a more modest $26,000 a year, or $500 a week. Translation: barely enough. Meantime, I'm happy to report, her credit cards are used responsibly and paid off in good time. And somehow, Amy's discovered ways to afford Italian-made shoes, organic carrots, and a stock trading at more than $600 a share.

But when you meet Amy at happy hour, go shopping with her, or work next to her cube, you get it. For one, when it comes to money, Amy's got moxie. Bravada. Or, as her Israeli father would say, chutzpah. She's fierce. (Incidentally, I don't suggest debating a woman's right to choose or the athletic prowess of the Penn State football team with Amy, especially when she's on her second Ketel One and tonic.) Second, Amy has a healthy relationship with money. She values it just like her close friendships, her career path, her law-school grades, and, most of all, her integrity. Amy is also, very importantly, in control of her needs and knows what she wants in hierarchical order to achieve her crafted version of the so-called good life. She's not anal. She's decisive.

And here's the best part—Amy is just like you and me. I swear! It may not seem so, what with her fancy footwear and first-class flights. (Fellas, you can change her name to Andrew and replace her pumps with a sweet flat screen and her Ketel One with that mouthwatering $45 /case of beer from the microbrewery in town.) The point is that Amy is no stranger to our legion of young, self-made professionals. We, too, are savvy, opinionated, and oh-so fierce. She, like us, lives in the Information Age and is excellent at making educated choices (big thanks to Google and episodes of *Oprah*). And all that has and will continue to serve as fuel for Amy's financial freedom—more so than her $500-a-week paycheck.

Why are so few of the rest of us able to apply our righteous attitudes to our wallets? It's the question every personal finance book for the young and moneyless has attempted to answer. It usually goes like this, "Slaves to debt, living paycheck to paycheck, credit card to credit card, a tragic and growing number of single twenty- and thirty-somethings have little if any financial cushion." What seems more serious is the apparent lack of empowerment essential to change, to dig ourselves out of financial misery. My own money "issues" have been and sometimes continue to be the following (raise your hand if this is you): an inability to delay gratification, a mad desire for all things Hollywood prescribes (and by *Hollywood*, I mean Jennifer Aniston), and a false feeling of protection when pulling out the plastic (credit cards, not condoms).

And, as I've heard from successful, hardworking baby boomers (i.e., our parents and bosses), we have a ridiculous sense of entitlement that justifies a pair of $400 Oliver Peoples shades. *But c'mon, they are amazing! Plus, they make me look thinner, so there.*

Finance empress Suze Orman and company would say this is just one of the endless examples of our financial incompetence. Suze may have the know-how, and millions of Americans subscribe to her get-real, no-fuss advice. But for me and probably many of you, it doesn't resonate. I want to enjoy spending money and not be reprimanded for it. According to the personal finance shelf at Barnes and Noble, we're doomed because (1) we're weak and vulnerable, (2) creditors will take advantage of our naïveté and our lack of financial education, and (3) we're selfish and gluttonous. The advice is ridden with tsk-tsks and tends to make us feel miserable for buying things we're not "worthy" of. The general financial advice is also, from what I've gathered, too cold-turkey, at least for me. I don't know about you, but I just can't cut up my Visa. And who can feasibly eat canned tuna for a year? A *week?* Maybe.

Instead, I, Farnoosh, because I'm right there with you, know you salivate for that video iPod and you're going to buy it no matter what—preferably in limited-edition red. So why not help you get it for less, while, at the same time, describe how *else* to better manage your money and, as it may be, piles (and piles) of debt? Although we may not have been born as financially savvy as Amy, we can certainly learn to be. I did. Now for you, it might not have to be the hard way.

And all right, yes, for the record, I do agree with Suze on a few points. Our generation gorges on material stuff and buys way too much on credit. I have made some pretty dumb financial moves, too—big and small, starting right during college when I'd use my ATM receipt as a trusted financial adviser. "Well, it says I have a hundred and twenty dollars left in my checking account. Chocolate cake shots for everyone!" I bounced checks, paid bills late, and bought cashmere sweaters I couldn't technically afford. I see many of my friends—superbright, impressively independent, former valedictorians, career leaders, determined, ambitious—in thousands and thousands of dollars of credit-card debt.

We overspend when we don't have to and we neglect to invest in our future. Our day-to-day financial obstacles (e.g., rent, gas, food) often hinder our ability to think and act big and beyond (e.g., retirement, investing, buying a home, erasing debt).

But here's where my approach is different. I say we can change and we don't have to get rid of our wants. How about applying our smarts, ambitions, and good looks to getting more for less? That's right, I said good looks—you know you're hot. So here's my promise: In this book, you can learn how to save and how to have enough money for your double-shot latte. You can learn how to spend and splurge smart. And oh yeah, you can learn how to shed your debt in good time. You'll even get the hang of what those talking heads on CNBC and Fox Business are gabbing about. Jim Cramer breaks it down in his part on investing (see chapter 7). And all this, without a lecture, without making you feel guilty or unworthy or desperate. You're going to get to live your life, maintain your desire for life's luxuries, be fiscally responsible, and learn ways to live beyond your means but spend *within* them.

It's true—money may not buy happiness, but having no money isn't exactly paradise, either. Having *some* cash but managing it poorly is nearly as bad. Then you're missing out on your money's potential to ameliorate the quality of your life. How we deal with our hard-earned money, how we spend it, save it, earn and burn it inevitably affects our lives and our futures. So we better learn to develop a healthy relationship now, when we're young and tough, when we've the energy and sharp motor skills to defend our money and our livelihoods.

When push comes to shove and that annoying salesman at Circuit City won't stop asking you to sign up for a store credit card (but you'll get 10 percent off your purchase, sir!), tell him who's in charge. Tell him and every other force tugging at your platinum Gucci money clip that you're better than that. You're smarter than that. You, my friend, are so money.

CHAPTER 1

LIFE. IS. GOOD.

No, really. It is. Keep reading.

Trying to define *good*, as in *the good life*, is like asking someone to define *success*. It varies by person. For some, *the good life* may
mean a high-powered career, two and a half kids, and a log-cabin
getaway. For others it's staying single, working just three days a
week, and having an unlimited supply of Rolling Rock in the
fridge. My own shifting definition of *the good life* has taken me
through different jobs, hairstyles, and zip codes, even more frequently now as I journey through my twenties. And rightly so, I
think. That's because our perspectives on life and our version of
the good life change as we experience it. But I wonder if our core
values ever really vanish. Things like family, career, friendships,
and, above all, our self-respect.

I never thought much about money or how I'd manage it before I started to make some for myself, but I always valued the
idea of money and how it equated to financial security. That was
mostly thanks to being raised by immigrant parents, a mother and
father who, in their early twenties, moved to the United States
from rural Iran with just a few suitcases and the keys to a one-
bedroom apartment in Worcester, Massachusetts. Until I was two

years old, my parents and I lived off of my dad's $480 monthly teaching stipend while he earned his PhD in physics ($180 went toward monthly rent; the rest probably went to diapers and milk). Still, somehow, my parents managed to throw frequent and full-course dinner parties for fellow married graduate-school students. The secret, my mother would tell me years later, was fast-washing the dishes and glasses after each course to make it look like they had enough tableware. Sometimes she'd borrow wineglasses from the neighbor downstairs. Not to mention, in true Persian style, Mom successfully haggled with the local butcher to be able to amply serve all five couples.

My sitter during these soirees was Nora, the eighty-one-year-old grandmother on the second floor who wouldn't accept money from my mom. Instead my mom would cook her home-made Persian food. For my mom it was a bona fide no-brainer way to save on child care. Nora and her husband, Frank, taught me lessons about money, too, come to think of it. For example, weekday evenings they'd feast on inexpensive microwave TV dinners (a fascinating thing at age four), choosing to splurge instead on trips up and down the East Coast in their shiny Cadillac to visit all nine of their grandchildren. They always brought them presents. And Nora's candy jar was always filled with fresh Tootsie Rolls.

All this is to say that before you can finance your "good life," you have to figure out what "good" means to you. The point is to find out what you value the most and what it is that makes you the happiest. Sometimes it helps to reminisce on those wonder years when your instincts were probably spot-on. I remember day-dreaming at the age of twelve of all the things I would be and as-pired to do when I was on my own. I was wrong about some things, of course. For example, I imagined I'd be married with kids by twenty-seven. (Note: Sixth graders in 1992 suffered from severe age inflation; back then twenty-seven was like forty and beyond today.) I also thought I was going to live in a suburb, but since graduating from college, Manhattan's been my home. And despite majoring in finance, I opted to be a journalist, not a banker.

In my version of the good life, I always planned to be career oriented. No matter what the job, I sensed I'd be extremely consumed by work. I always suspected I was a family person (though, ladies, not always cool to admit on the first date). But yes, I want to be a mom someday. I also knew I'd seek higher education beyond college. That may have been more of a parental influence, as my parents placed a great deal of emphasis and importance on education during my childhood. To them, it raised your status in society and earned you more money. Mom taught herself English and finally graduated from college in her mid-twenties while raising me at home. Good grades were not an option; they would be my ticket to financial security, she often reminded me.

Me: *"Mom! Ninety-seven on the math test!"*

Mom: *"What happened to the other three points?"*

Me: *Sigh.*

That crazy study and work ethic found me taking on twenty-four credits (eight classes) and three jobs (waitressing, telemarketing, and selling ads for the college paper) during my sophomore year in college. Friday nights were too often spent filing internship applications for the following summer. I apparently don't remember it being *that* extreme, but my roommate at the time and best friend, Kate, remembers it quite well, arriving back at the dorm at 2 A.M. from downtown bars to find me with my nose in Corporate

Finance 401. That said, Kate's social life didn't hold her back; she is a highly successful journalist in New York City. A closet studier? Actually, come to think of it, Kate is a tremendous smarty-pants, so she probably didn't need as much time with her head stuck in a textbook as I did.

But don't get me wrong. I worked hard and I *played* hard. I was cool! Really! Which brings me to my other good-life variable: a social life. I enjoy going out with friends and sipping adult beverages (preferably together). I won't divulge on these pages, but let's just say you had to be there. My friendships are tremendously important to me, and I thrive on getting out there and discovering new opportunities, new ideas, and great fun.

Still another variable in my good-life algorithm is clothing. Pretty clothes. And I know I want to invest in more real estate down the road. It's a top priority since I can't trade individual stocks—my job as a financial journalist prohibits it. So, real estate is how I've chosen to "invest" my money. I started in 2004 by buying a studio apartment in Manhattan. I was making only $46,600 a year at the time. (How did I do it? You'll have to find out in chapter 8.)

My good life also requires financial security. To that end, I need to save or invest (except in stocks) or both. Ever heard of the expression *Pay yourself first?* Throughout this book you'll see there are ways to reward yourself financially, aside from saving at the cash register. There are ways, for example, to make more money out of money. Just taking a shaving off your paycheck and storing it in a security—be it stocks, a 401(k) plan, or a high-yield savings account—will lead to (poof!) a substantial accumulation of money over a period of time. How you use that savings is up to you. Right now I have an ING direct savings account that I've been stashing 5 percent of my monthly paycheck in over the past two years. Thanks to the bit of interest the account offers, my "Rainy Day" fund is well on its way to paying for a relaxing week-long vacation in South America, including flight, four-star hotel room, and all-I-can-drink margaritas. Or, it could pay for two months of sitting on my couch in case I lose my job. Personally, I'm rooting for Buenos Aires.

And, of course, I want to live a healthy life. I hope that's in everyone's good-life equation. It ought to be a fixed variable. But unfortunately, staying healthy in America requires, to a degree, proper medical attention, which is far from cheap and ironically unaffordable sometimes for those who need it the most. I've devoted a whole chapter to the topic of health care and how to better survive this financial burden, as it's become. (See chapter 12 for more on this.)

So that's my basic good life (for at least the next five to seven years): a successful career, a family (someday), money in the bank, my health, a busy social life, a city address (among others), and a closet full of Diane von Furstenberg apparel. Current DVF wrap-dress count: 3. Babies: 0. And that makes me really happy.

I'm sure we've all done this equation in our head more or less. Or, if we haven't, maybe it's time we did. Because how else will we be able to make smart financial choices? How else will we be able to be financially independent and live life to the fullest of our expectations? If money doesn't *directly* buy happiness, it does buy stuff that we wear, live in, drive, and eat. It pays for our education. It pays for our comfort. And those things contribute to our happiness, right?

YOUR NEED-WANTS, AKA THE MUST-HAVES

In examining your good life, there is no need for superspecifics. You don't need to think too long term, either, although more power to you if you can boil it all down to the day when you are playing chess with your new friend Saul at the pool in Boca Raton. But whatever you throw into that good-life equation, make sure you don't forget the "need-wants." A need-want is outside Maslow's hierarchy. That means the stuff outside of our actual survival needs like air, basic food, water, friendship, (sex?). Instead, it's a *want* in theory and a *need* in the reality of your good life (like my DVF wrap dresses and NYC zip code). I suppose I can wear a faux wrap and live in Hoboken and still "exist," but I would be miserable.

Figuring out our hierarchy of true need-wants is extremely important as we evaluate our financial lives and how we ultimately allocate our money. From there, the next step is learning how to maximize those need-wants with less money. After all, it's not the survival needs that get us into money trouble; I don't know too many people who purposely splurge on rent or water or air-conditioning. Rather, it's the plasma TVs, gizmos, gadgets, and $6 Häagen-Dazs cones that seem like needs at the time but have us waking up and saying, "Crap! I don't have enough money for lunch!" or "Can I put my soy caramel latte on Visa?"

Once you've identified your need-wants, extraneous expenses like renting an overcrowded summer house with friends and buying organic detergent, once purchased with little brain action, may seem superfluous and unnecessary when you realize where *else* your money can go to better satisfy your ideal life, both for today and the next day.

My friend Lee once told me in college, "Everyone can drive a Mercedes, Farnoosh. It just depends on how badly you want it." And no, he didn't suggest hot-wiring a Benz. He meant that the good life equates to having a will and finding a way. You may gladly cut out a daily latte and HBO to ensure buying a crisp, new Paul Smith shirt every month because your advertising director boss won't promote you if you're wearing anything from the Gap. Or you may be an extreme sports enthusiast who would rather buy the new BMX bike than a new Mac notebook. Or you may, indeed, fill up on canned tuna for a few years in order to buy a Benz on a middle-school teacher's salary. Crazier things have happened!

Of course, as a disclaimer, your good life won't be possible without taking responsibility for those actual survival needs I listed earlier. You can't ignore outstanding loans and car payments, and those are the things we address first in this book. No one likes to get a call from a collection agent or come home to an eviction notice. Your needs should always include a savings and/or investing variable, too. It may seem impossible to save with a limited income, but it's not. If it pains you so, I've got ways to save that won't bite. I promise—just keep reading.

And that's the last bit of mommying from me. From here on out, it's sassy Aunt Farnoosh, the chick who comes to family functions in skinny heels, gets drunk off gin martinis, and is crazy for the word *fabulous*. She inspires you to take chances and occasionally slips you a $50—way more than nerdy Uncle Jed, who takes pride in his dollar-coin give-outs. On a separate note, would someone please forward him the 1988 memo about no longer combining socks with Teva sandals? The Air Jesus look is so over.

➤ ➤ ➤ ➤ Your Hierarchy of Need-Wants . . . in Half an Hour

Here are some questions, some short-term, others more long-term, to help you prescribe your need-wants for the good life. It all boils down to isolating the necessary ingredients for your ideal lifestyle. Who knows? I'm willing to bet that your answers stem from those so-called values we talked about earlier in this chapter.

Do I like kids? And not other people's kids. Kids of my own?
City or suburb?

SUV or Prius? Or subway? Walk? Segway?

Do I want to retire early and play chess with Saul or open a Dunkin' Donuts at sixty-five?

How often do I want to travel?

Do I want to go to graduate school?

Can I stand living with a roommate?

Designer or designer-imposter?

Do I prefer a book in bed on Saturday night or to party like a rock star?

Fine wine or bottled beer? Or both?

FM or satellite radio? NPR?

Will I freelance or be on staff? Or both?

Can I cook? Do I prefer eating out?

Do I ever want to start my own business?

Goldfish or golden retriever? Or both?

Big, fancy wedding or small, backyard ceremony? Elope?

Will I mooch off my parents for a few more years or rent my own place now?

Do I want to be a homeowner in the next few years?

Do I want to quit my job soon?

THE WALLET WORKOUT

Once you have a better sense of your preferred lifestyle, take a look at your *actual* paycheck, which, if you work for a full-time employer, reflects deductions for things like taxes, health care, Social Security, and perhaps your 401(k) retirement account. What's left is your "disposable income"—what's technically in your wallet—and what you'll end up using mostly to pay for your needs (fixed expenses). Whatever's left after that you get to spend on your need-wants (variable expenses). Hooray!

Exercise 1: The Tax Crunch

One slice of your paycheck just has to go to Uncle Sam, unless you enjoy wearing stripes and making license plates that read DADZGRL. Taxes have been around in America since the Pilgrims and they're not going anywhere. They are a fixed cost (i.e., there's no negotiating) and typically round out to be 25 to 30 percent of your paycheck. Ouch. The only other item in your life right now that eats that much pie is probably your rent or mortgage. The biggest chunk of your taxes typically goes to the federal government. This includes income tax (to pay for new bridges and presidential balls), Social Security (so the gov't can pretend it's going to pay you a monthly stipend one day), and Medicare (to help pay for your Viagra at sixty-seven). In the illustrations, I left out taxes because your employer already takes that out of your gross income. What's left is your net earnings, the money we aim to stretch!

➤ ➤ ➤ ➤ Dealing with Uncle Sam

My editor, Lindsay, said I needed to include something on how to pay your taxes because that's something she struggled with (and me, as well). And she's supersmart, so you know there have to be millions more who have no clue about how or where to begin. Here's the skinny on taxes and why, for most of us law-abiding citizens, they're not as scary as IRS auditors make them out to be.

1. Check your mail vigilantly in January. "Tax statements" should arrive this month from the various agencies that paid you in the previous year or agencies to which you paid taxes. You'll know from the envelopes because they'll usually say "Important Tax Forms Enclosed." (Duh!) Expect mail from your employer, your student loan organization, your municipality (if you paid real estate taxes), and maybe even your bank plus any other firms where you have investments (if you earned interest on any savings or dividends and capital gains/losses on any investments). *Keep all these statements in a secure place.* You'll need them again in a month or so when you crack open the IRS tax claim forms. If you think you're missing a tax statement from one of these agencies, call them and ask what is up! Even after filing your return, *keep the tax forms and all your statements for three years, in case the IRS comes knocking for an audit.*

2. Gather up all your donation receipts. Any donations you made to Goodwill, the Salvation Army, or another qualified charitable organization in the previous year can help reduce your taxable income! And P.S. Helping a good cause is an awesome way to reduce your taxable income.

3. For some: Free file. If your individual gross income for the year is below a certain amount, you qualify for the IRS's Free File program, which essentially means you pay nothing to get your taxes filed online. Visit www.irs.gov/efile for more.

4. For everyone else: Have at least $100 stashed for tax season (usually the deadline lurks around April 15). The good news is we can file our taxes online these days, which saves the hassle of going to the local tax-prep office and waiting in line for hours. The unfortunate news is many of us still need to *pay* to get our taxes done. Whether you do it online through Turbo Tax or go to H&R Block, it's going to cost you. It costs less to log onto Turbo Tax, where there's no actual human interaction, roughly $30 to $75 depending on which tax-filing program you choose. But there is an advantage to working with an actual human tax expert. (See the next numbered point.)

5. Get help. If you're still not sure how to do your taxes and would like to learn the basics, I do recommend sitting down *with a professional tax* *preparer or maybe even an older friend* who's done his or her taxes for a few years in order to get more comfortable with the process. My first year with a full-time job, I journeyed over to H&R Block with all my tax forms. In two hours the nice lady had sent off my tax filings to the IRS (I nodded, pretending to fully understand). The best part about the experience was that she gave me a copy of all my IRS forms that she had filled out. The following year I just filed my taxes solo using last year's forms as a reference point. So far, I'm audit free. At H&R Block, Jackson Hewitt, and the rest, be prepared to pay anywhere from $75 and upward, depending on the extensiveness of your tax filings.

6. Have all your forms by your side if you go solo and attempt to file your taxes online. With the nature of e-filing programs, the key is organization and knowing how to connect the dots. Don't be scared by all the IRS mumbo jumbo like Form 1040 or Schedule C-EZ. Also, don't think you have to do it all in one sitting. You can do it here and there whenever you have the patience and time. Online programs will save your last entry and pick up where you left off.

7. Tip for freelancers. Finally, for those who work freelance or have side gigs apart from their nine-to-fives, keep all receipts for meals, travel, entertainment, computer, printer, camera, etc., that relate to your freelance work. That's generally all tax deductible. If you use your home as an office, you can also deduct part of your rent or mortgage from your taxable income. Again, keep these receipts for three years in case the IRS wants to verify that you, in fact, work where you sleep, or that $80 lunch with a "source" did, in fact, occur with another person.

Exercise 2: The Retirement Push-up

This should be treated as a need, although we live so much in the present that we often forget about the golden years. Or perhaps more accurately, we neglect them because it seems like there's plenty of time to save later, especially when you feel like you're living paycheck to paycheck now. Remember: Social Security is not all it was cut out to be, and our generation is likely to receive little if any money from the government. Pensions are also fast evaporating, leaving individuals the even bigger burden of getting their act together by retirement. So starting to save even the minimum amount your company will match in a 401(k) retirement account is so important. So, say, if your company agrees to match 50 percent of your 401(k) investment up to 10 percent of your salary, take advantage of that. Laying down 10 percent of your salary, which let's say is $5,000, may earn you a free $2,500. And that $5,000 doesn't have to go down in one big chunk. It's taken out of each paycheck, which is a lot less painful. Before you know it, you have the beginnings of a sweet nest egg. It sure beats waking up at forty-five and wishing you'd been saving and growing that money for the last twenty years! Rather, you can look forward to the joy of not having to get up for work and instead attending clay pottery classes on Tuesdays and Thursdays at the Jewish Community Center. Fantastic.

So how to get your savings engines going for sixty-five and beyond? 401(k)s and individual retirement accounts, or IRAs, are probably the easiest solutions. Financial experts agree that during your twenties and thirties, if you're single and independent, your 401(k) contribution should be at least 10 percent of your annual gross income. If 10 percent is a total stretch, you should at least contribute what your employer *matches*. Both 401(k)s and IRAs have annual caps, limiting how much you can contribute. It changes every year, so just double-check with your human resources department. Totally lost? Here's more on 401(k)s and IRAs.

The 401(K), aka Free Money

If you work for a decent employer, you should have access to a 401(k) account, which companies often sponsor on behalf of money-management firms. It's named after a section of the Internal Revenue Code, in case you need factoids to kill time on the date from hell.

A 401(k) basically lets you defer some of your paycheck to a savings account that can grow by being invested in various mutual funds, bonds, and stocks. The bummer is you can't withdraw the 401(k) money from the account until you turn sixty-five, or you face annoying fees. On the flip side, the allocation is automatic, so you never have to actually write a check and send off your money sobbingly. And by dedicating some of your paycheck to a 401(k) plan, you reduce your taxable income, so the government essentially takes away less of your money.

What's more—ever heard that a 401(k) is like free money? That's actually true in many cases: At many companies, the employer will match your contribution up to a certain percentage point. When I worked at Time Warner, the company would match roughly two-thirds of my contribution up to something like 10 or 12 percent. So for every dollar I deferred to the account, Time Warner would throw in an extra sixty-seven cents, more or less. Not too shabby. (I also got free cable and Internet, but got completely low-balled when it came to salary. Trade-offs, I guess!) But here's the reality: In just three years, I saved $25,000 for retirement!

➤ ➤ ➤ ➤ Your 401(k) Fixings . . . in an Hour

Your work's not done after telling HR you want part of your paycheck distributed to the employer-sponsored 401(k) plan. You then have to pick and choose which mutual funds or stocks you want your 401(k) plan invested in. Now, you can't pick just anything, like one hundred shares of Google, please. Instead, the company should provide you with a list of about fifteen to twenty choices, which usually include your company's stock and a range of unfamiliar mutual funds. You then are asked to make your allocations (e.g., 10 percent to XYZ mutual fund, 12.5 percent to a bond fund, 40 percent to company stock, etc.).

That said, you're not likely to be familiar with the options, minus the company's stock. A good rule of thumb is to spread your allocation broadly, so you don't expose yourself to too much risk if, say, the company's stock plummets or XYZ mutual fund goes under. In other words, diversify. Pick at least five different funds, in addition to your company's stock if you like, and allocate 10 to 20 percent to each fund and a bit less to your company's stock. You can distribute your money to even more funds if you want super diversification. As for which funds to choose, that's almost like throwing darts. But, look for words like *international, money market, municipal,* and *small-cap, large-cap,* and *mid-cap.* Choose at least one of each to get exposure to overseas markets, the domestic money market, the bond market, and small to large companies.

Second, you can always pop open your laptop and go to a number of sites to see each fund's rate of return or how much they gained year-to-date. Each mutual fund has a ticker, which the list usually includes. For example, the Fidelity Advisor International Small Cap Opportunity fund (ticker: FOPAX), according to free info sites like finance.yahoo.com or finance.google.com, says the fund invests in relatively small foreign companies. Year-to-date it's earned more than 9 percent. Not bad. In general, don't sweat the funds. Just invest in a good variety so that, again, you don't get creamed if a single fund goes belly up, which is a rarity. A bigger risk is investing more than 10 or 15 percent of your 401(k) money in your company's stock. Take it from many of Enron's former employees. Or even my former coworkers at Time Warner, who saw their company's stock plummet from a high of $71/share to a low of about $9/share during the worst of times, the failed merger with AOL.

What If I Leave My Job? If you switch jobs, whether on good terms or bad, the 401(k) savings is still yours to keep. Or at least *your* contribution to it is. Most companies can take back their contributions if you haven't been there long enough for the money to be vested (i.e., actually yours), a time span that varies by company but usually happens after three to five years of employment. The best thing to do is to roll over the money to your next employer's 401(k) manager. Don't skip the sidebar on how to properly switch over a 401(k) account. It can cost you money if you're not careful! I've also got a nifty sidebar that takes a closer look at how to *select* your 401(k) distribution.

➤ ➤ ➤ ➤ **Stop, Drop, and Roll Over Your 401(k) . . . in an Hour**

If you permanently leave your job (and by the way, isn't that the best feeling?) and you have a 401(k) account, your plan administrator (Fidelity or Merrill Lynch, for example) must provide a written explanation of your options thirty to ninety days before the deadline to take action. Those options are:

Do nothing. While this isn't the recommended option, it can be helpful, if, say, you're desperate for the money because you'll be unemployed for a long while, your rent is going up, or you will be freelancing and need some starter income to help you out. This is officially known as automatic distribution. Your 401(k) manager automatically cashes out your 401(k) and sends you a check in the mail. But unless you're sixty-five, you'll face heavy taxes, since this is considered an early withdrawal from your 401(k).

Roll over to a new 401(k). Here's the recommended approach. If your new employer offers a 401(k) savings plan, transfer your account directly to your new employer's managing institution. For example, when I went from NY1 News to thestreet.com, my managing institution switched from Fidelity to UST Trust. Make sure to act fast. I know starting a new job is overwhelming with so much paperwork, and you can easily forget all about your 401(k) plan. Just talk to your new human resources rep about your situation and he or she will give you the proper paperwork to facilitate the switcheroo. The money is transferred automatically. You'll likely get a notice in the mail about it.

Note: Make sure to check in with your new managing institution a few months after the switch . . . just to make *SURE* the money is there. A lot of times you can just check online at their Web site or call their 1-800 number. I only say this because I checked my new 401(k) balance eight months after working at thestreet.com only to discover the old money wasn't there! A quick visit to HR helped. We discovered after a few phone calls that the money was "in limbo," just hanging out at the new managing institution's reserves without being in its proper home (read: my account). Can you believe it? I had sacrificed 10 percent of my income for three years for this alleged "retirement savings vehicle" and if I wasn't keeping an eye on someone else's job, the money could have really disappeared. Along those lines, keep a good paper trail of all letters, account statements, and notices from your 401(k) account manager and any money manager for at least two years, be it a bank or your company's financial office. You never know!

Roll over to an IRA. If you've yet to get a new job, are going full-time freelance, or your new employer doesn't offer a 401(k) plan, consider shifting your account to an IRA. Again, do a direct rollover to avoid the hefty taxes.

The IRA (Not the Irish Republican Army)

Still another retirement vehicle that works well for us youngins is an IRA, or individual retirement account. An IRA is popular, mostly because of its substantial tax benefits. Like a 401(k), your IRA money can be invested in various financial instruments to help the money grow faster than if it was just sitting under your mattress. Anyone under age 72½ can open an IRA, and, like a 401(k), you get slapped with a penalty for an early withdrawal. In this case, an early withdrawal is before age fifty-nine.

There are two types of IRAs: traditional and Roth. Sites like www.statefarm.com and www.jpmorganinvest.com offer online calculators to help determine the best IRA for you. Here's a basic rundown of each.

Traditional IRAs. Traditional IRAs offer tax-deferred growth. In other words, you pay taxes on your investment gains only when you make withdrawals during retirement (remember, in the IRA world, retirement eligibility is age fifty-nine). Every year the federal government sets limits on the maximum contribution to a certain dollar amount or percentage of an individual's earned income per year, whichever is less. Annual contributions are tax deductible. This form of IRA works best for those who need the tax deduction right now, or if you expect to pay fewer taxes when you retire. With traditional accounts, there's also a slap on the wrist for not withdrawing money soon enough. You usually need to begin taking money from your traditional IRA no later than April 1 of the calendar year following the date you reach age 72½.

Roth IRAs. By contrast, Roth IRAs grow tax free. This is the favored IRA option for people in our generation. Although the annual contributions are not tax deductible, you owe no tax when you make withdrawals in retirement. Annual contribution limits are the same as those for traditional IRAs. (Note: Not everyone qualifies for a Roth IRA account. Individuals with an adjusted gross income, or AGI, of more than $95,000 can't take part, nor can joint filers with an AGI of more than $150,000.) Early earnings withdrawals from a Roth IRA are generally taxable and also subject to a 10 percent penalty.

Exercise 3: The Rainy-Day Indoor Mile

This is all about y-o-u. Give yourself some love. Having money for a rainy day or cash emergency is a true measure of financial freedom. As David Bach, one of my favorite money experts often says, pay yourself first! Take at least 10 percent of your paycheck and automatically put it toward an interest-earning savings account. If not 10 percent, then at least something so you can start getting used to saving. As a rule of thumb, you should aim to have at least three to six months of income saved in case of an emergency, like losing your job or having to help pay for a serious medical bill. High-yielding online savings accounts are one option. I'll get more into how to make the most of your rainy-day savings further on in the book.

Exercise 4: The Home Stretch

Rent should not really exceed 30 percent of your net earnings. But for those of us living in big cities with inflated real estate (e.g., New York, San Francisco, Boston, to name a few), some of us have to go as high as 40 percent just to live in a place with a window and running water. It's also not unheard of, in those aforementioned cities, to dedicate one bimonthly paycheck a month or more to rent. You've also got utilities to cover—another 2 to 5 percent of your paycheck. Owning a home may reduce your monthly cash outflow dramatically, but buying property takes some serious planning and supersaving. Remember, it can be done if you're willing (chapter 8 gives you the ins and outs).

Exercise 5: Diet

Food is a must! This can be an adjustable cost, depending on whether you desire to cook or need to eat on the go. Figure at least 10 percent of your paycheck will account for groceries and another 10 to 15 percent for meals out.

Excerise 6: Cheat (Or, Satisfy Your Need-Wants, the Miscellaneous)

Now that you've covered your needs, you can spring for your need-wants. At this point, you're probably left with somewhere between 5 and 10 percent of your disposable income (and that might be generous). Financial experts call this miscellaneous spending, and it includes clothing, concert tickets, etc. Throughout this book we'll face these desires head on and show how you can get what you want, when you want it, at the price you can afford.

➤ ➤ ➤ ➤ What's in Your Wallet?

I've illustrated some examples of working out a wallet (already taking into account taxes and any employee-sponsored retirement savings and health care when available through an employee-sponsored plan). All characters are fictional. Any likeness to actual people is purely coincidental.

P.S. These percentages are rough. If you attempt to do this at home with your own paycheck, realize that it's almost impossible to be 100 percent accurate. The point is not to get mathematical, but to stimulate thought, to get you looking realistically at your needs and your must-haves. And maybe (hopefully) get you to laugh a little.

1. Beyoncé, a twenty-three-year-old junior analyst on Wall Street, aspiring chef, and all-around diva

Needs: rent, food, savings, college loan, utilities, subway card, cell phone, health care

Need-wants: French-cuff shirts, Mauviel copper cookware set, adult beverages on weekends, dinners out, yoga classes

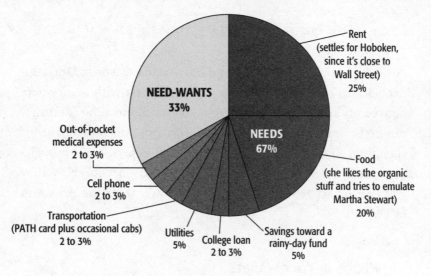

2. Ashton, a twenty-nine-year-old freelance video editor in San Diego, aspiring film producer, and wannabe surfer pro

Needs: car payment and insurance, rent, food, health care, savings, utilities, gas, cell phone

Need-wants: new Mobley custom longboard, PS3 games, film workshops, iTunes downloads

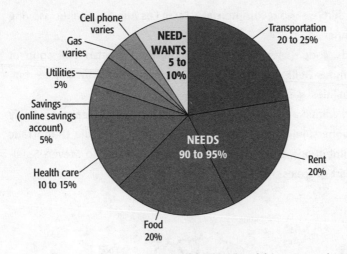

Cell phone
varies

Gas
varies

Utilities
5%

Savings
(online savings
account)
5%

Health care
10 to 15%

**NEED-
WANTS
5 to
10%**

Transportation
20 to 25%

**NEEDS
90 to 95%**

Rent
20%

Food
20%

3. Angelina, a twenty-six-year-old high school history teacher, working to pay off her college credit-card debt and apply to the Peace Corps, still lives at home

Needs: credit-card payment, car payment and insurance, eating out (Mom cooks, so food is always aplenty, but dining out gets her out of the house), savings, cell phone, gas

Need-wants: Coachella tickets, gym membership, Starbucks triple-shot mocha Frappuccinos

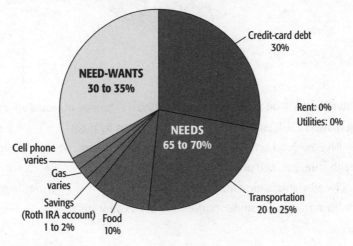

**NEED-WANTS
30 to 35%**

Credit-card debt
30%

Rent: 0%
Utilities: 0%

**NEEDS
65 to 70%**

Cell phone
varies

Gas
varies

Savings
(Roth IRA account)
1 to 2%

Food
10%

Transportation
20 to 25%

4. Leo, a thirty-year-old commercial actor in Los Angeles, waiter, aspiring Oscar winner

Needs: food (especially late-night bowls of matzo ball soup at Jerry's Famous Deli), car payment and insurance, health insurance, rent, savings, utilities, gas, cell phone

Need-wants: adult beverages, club covers, designer jeans, biweekly trips to tanners, jujitsu classes, personal training, charitable Democratic Party contributions, Scientology membership, the key to Steven Spielberg's heart (priceless)

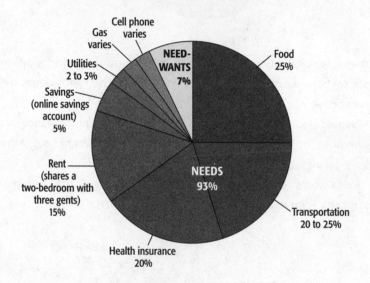

5. Avril, a thirty-one-year-old assistant district attorney in Houston, aspiring Marsha Clark, and cover band frontwoman by night

Needs: food, car payment and insurance, rent, savings, utilities, health care, gas, cell phone (er, crackberry)

Need-wants: suits, mani/pedis, Manolo Blahniks, gourmet ingredients to host weekly dinner parties, acoustic guitar strings

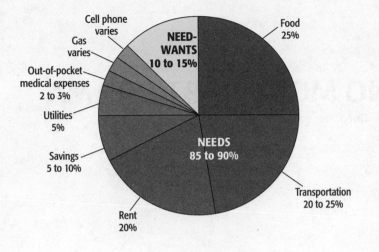

CHAPTER 2

NO MORE DEBT DRAMA
The Good, the Bad, the Fugly

When my Chemistry 102 partner Dustin graduated from college in 2003, he got behind his Hyundai Sonata and drove cross-country to Tinseltown with little in his trunk but a suitcase and a draft of what he still hopes will be his first hit screenplay. Like fellow grads, he left Penn State with hopes, dreams, and a high tolerance for alcohol. Nothing was going to get in his way— not even his $23,000 in federal loans. So he did what any smart, forward-looking college grad would do. He ditched the debt for a good five years.

That's the surprising thing about this ugly four-letter word *debt*: Sometimes it can actually work in our favor. A mortgage, for example, is pretty impressive debt. It certainly beats paying rent. Student loans are also good, relatively speaking. Having one shows a financial dedication to education, and creditors *get* that. (Everyone knows higher education comes at an extremely high price these days, so credit-rating agencies typically perceive student loans as favorable debt, so long as you pay the minimum monthly balance on time and in good faith.) What's more, unlike credit-card debt, which is downright fugly, student loans and home mortgages have relatively low interest rates, so they're not as financially dire as credit cards. Not to mention, a Stafford loan may ultimately help you earn a degree and land work, but mooching off Visa and paying just the minimum balance month to month gets no respect—and rightfully so.

If you have no debt, you're ahead of the game and your friends probably hate you.

For everyone else, keep reading to learn how to reduce and pay off your debt from, say, that leftover Perkins loan to, as it may be, your four-figure Visa bill.

The nutshell advice on debt: Just deal with it. Kick its ass. Because nothing feels worse than realizing you've barely enough cash in your checking account to pay the minimum balance on your credit card or other loans. Trust me, dealing with debt is much better than the alternative: staying up during the night, doing the awful math in your head . . . *Wonder if I still have the receipt to those headphones? That was so stupid. I mean a hundred bucks?? All I needed was a pack of AAA batteries. Maybe if I return the headphones! I'll be able to put that money toward my student loan this month. Brilliant!*

Next day: *Sorry, ma'am, the store doesn't take back opened and used items. Is that peanut butter? And this was bought fifteen days ago. We have a strict no-cash-back return policy after fourteen days. Just exchanges. Also, please stop crying. How about a nice iPhone instead?*

Poor is *so* last season.

That was my old accounting method. Awful and often unreliable and counterintuitive and stupid. And it led to, at one point, more than $4,000 in credit-card debt. But I just dealt with it one day. I grabbed a number 2 pencil and a spiral notepad, wrote down my monthly income and how much I needed to spend in order to survive (e.g., rent, groceries, toilet paper, utilities, cell phone) and what of my usual discretionary expenditures I would be no less happy without. My gym membership got the temporary boot, replaced with free runs in the park and taking the stairs (some-times) to my then-fifth-floor apartment. I learned how to boil water and bought one of those nifty thermo mugs into which I poured my own freshly brewed coffee from home. Starbucks could shove it for a while. I also kept my credit card at home if I went shopping or out to eat. I just used my debit card and cash, which made it harder to splurge. Really. I prioritized, organized, and bought fewer gadgets. And I discovered, when we better manage our bills, we better manage our lives. At the least, we get more sleep. And that beauty rest is precious money saved buying tubs of Oil of Olay fifteen years from now. Fine, ten.

My lightbulb moment? I recall a phone call with my mom during my final month in grad school. I was twenty-three and or-ganizing plans to go to Iran and be a stringer for Newsweek In-ternational. I was going to be a die-hard international journalist, and Columbia would name a wing after me in forty years. Mean-time, my mother was explaining on the phone that my married twenty-something cousin had just begged his mom (my aunt) to bail him out of credit-card debt. He and his wife had piled on $28,000 in charges before their second year of marriage and couldn't get any bank to grant them a mortgage. "Can you believe that? How does one possibly get into *that* much debt?" my sweet, unknowing mother asked me. "And so young. It's so embarrass-ing," she went on and on. "You don't have any credit-card debt, do you, Farnoosh?"

"No way!" I professed, knowing full well that my $4,000 bal-ance left over from Penn State and the past nine months in New York was soon on its way to another zero if I didn't get my act to-gether. Of course I *could* believe how a young couple could accumu-late so much plastic debt. It's not hard to spend money that doesn't technically exist. (If you don't see it, it doesn't exist, right?) Just like my old weight-obsessed friend Jen told me once during theater rehearsal in high school. "There's nothing wrong with eating other people's fries, Farnoosh. Other people's fries don't make you fat."

Jen is now a criminal defense attorney.

THE DEBT TOTEM POLE

Dealing with debt starts with figuring out where each outstanding loan sits on the debt totem pole. Think h-i-e-r-a-r-c-h-y. Traditionally, the loans you should deal with first, the ones up top, have the highest interest rates and aren't securitized. (Any debt like credit-card debt, store credit, etc., is not securitized because there's no asset to back up the money owed. The opposite would be a mortgage, which *is* securitized because if you default on your mortgage, the bank can take your house.) Toward the bottom of the totem pole sits the low-interest-rate debt and debt that is securitized, such as your car loan, your home mortgage, and student loans. These loans offer relatively more flexibility. (Note: I realize when I say home mortgage, I speak to just a fraction of readers out there. But I'm hoping chapter 8, "Homeward Bound," will help increase that percentage.)

PLASTIC, TOP OF THE TOTEM POLE

On average the U.S. consumer, according to some recent stats from www.cardtrak.com, carries just over $9,900 in credit-card debt. While that's less money than the average student loan, credit-card debt is by far more expensive to carry than a Perkins or Stafford loan because of the higher interest rates. The average annual percent yield, or APY, for a standard credit card is around 13 percent, compared to 7 or 8 percent on a student loan. The cards with the highest yields or rates should be your first concern because they're technically your most expensive loans. Like student loans, it may be worthwhile to consolidate your credit-card debt. In some cases you may find it helpful to transfer your balance on one card to another charging less interest. We'll explore these options here. And remember *options* is the key word. You have choices, and more than a few. It takes some moxie and logic to erase debt. And it goes without saying: To pay off the credit cards, you gotta stop using them.

Step 1: Ease the Interest

Gather up your credit cards and rank them by interest rate, highest to lowest. If you have just one card and have good credit, call up the credit-card company and ask for a lower rate. Throw into the conversation that you're considering transferring your balance to a different card company offering a lower rate. That usually does the trick. If you have *more* than one card, you will either want to consolidate or tackle each one separately. Multitacklers, make sure to read the next section.

Step 2: Size Up Your Cards

For those with numerous credit cards (i.e., two+), there are a few ways to manage the debt.

Let's picture this scenario with three credit cards and the following debt loads:

- ➤ $4,000 on credit-card 1 (leftover from college, APY 22 percent)
- ➤ $550 on department store card (last week's shopping binge, APY 18 percent)
- ➤ $1,000 on credit-card 2 (Spring Break 2007, APY 15 percent)

Step 3: Choose a Payoff Plan

Get High. One route to paying off credit-card debt is first paying off the card with the *highest* interest rate, or credit-card 1 in our above scenario. The logic: This is your most expensive account.

With a 22 percent APY, the longer you wait to pay it off, the more money it will cost you. This 22 percent APY card in our imaginary scenario also happens to have the highest balance. If it had the *smallest* balance, I'd still recommend paying it off first.

(Note: If your credit score is shot—as in below 600—this may not be the most recommended payoff method, especially if you need to buy a car or take on a bank loan of some sort. Why? Because for low credit-score bearers, it's paramount you reduce your debt-to-available-credit ratio as fast as possible, since you've the highest risk of getting refused for a car loan or student loan. Attack the debt that will be easiest to pay off first, doing whatever will quickly get you on track and in the habit of paying off all your debt. You may want to begin by paying off the card with the smallest balance, which I explain below, and working your way up.)

Start Small. Some may want to get rid of that $550 store credit-card debt before any other because it's the least daunting and offers a psychological boost. Attempting to erase $550 versus $4,000 of debt is a less discouraging way to get into payoff mode. From there, you could tackle the remaining two credit cards, again, either by the size of the debt or by APY.

Go to the Edge. If you're really close to maxing out one of your cards, pay off that one first. Reason is—you get penalized for getting too close to the limit on any credit card. Your interest rate might go up on that card and consequently other cards. Your credit score will also take a hit because, again, it's all about that debt-to-available-credit ratio. If you're using 90 percent of a credit card's limit, that's way too high. I've heard you don't want to use up more than 30 percent of a card's limit to avoid losing points on your credit score. So if that $1,000 balance is sitting on a card with a $1,500 max, you may want to start there first.

THANKS FOR DISCOVERING THIS AWESOME PAYOFF PLAN, SHERLOCK. NOW, HOW DO I COME UP WITH *MONEY* TO PAY OFF MY BALANCE(S)?

It's really easy for me to say how to *generally* devise a payoff plan for your credit cards. Don't get me wrong, all of the above is good advice and can and will help properly structure and organize your payment plan. But I know what you're wondering. How the heck do I pay off my balance? Where's the money supposed to come from? For me, I took advantage of any and all occasions that brought in extra money. Throughout the year, I'd pay off a little more than the minimum balance each month, whatever I could afford, and then come birthday, bonus, raise, and holiday gift-receiving time, I would use all the money I'd accumulated to substantially knock down the debt. My coworker Sheila had about $2,000 in credit-card debt coming out of college. She earned $29,000 working as an assistant in a law firm. In a year she wiped out the debt. How? A lot of ramen noodles and Chef Boyardee for a year and a $9 daily spending allowance, which left barely any opportunities to eat out or binge on beer. Still another perk to her spending crunch? Her financial diet helped her shed that freshman twenty.

It's not going to be fun paying off your credit-card bill. You'll have to use your money toward paying off your old purchases instead of on your normal routine spending ventures. It may mean cooking instead of ordering in or dining out for six months. It may mean giving up all your year-end bonus money to Visa or even moonlighting as a bartender two nights a week or babysitting (more on earning extra money toward the end of the book. Why doze off your active, vibrant, and able-bodied twenties when you could be making more money!). Just do everyone in our generation a favor, especially yourself—pay it off. Don't become another statistic.

CREDIT-CARD SHOPPING

Snail mail is such a novelty these days, but just when you get excited to see a small pile of envelopes in your mailbox (yay), you realize practically all are from credit-card companies (sigh). (A total of six billion card solicitations were sent out in 2006.) Your best move is to shred each and every one to avoid identity theft. But if you are in the market for a new card, there are some diamonds in the rough. Here's how to shop for a credit card.

Talk to Yourself. Ask yourself, *Self, why do I want a credit card? And how will I handle this card? Do I plan to pay off the balance each month? Or carry a balance? Do I want a new card to transfer my old debt?*

Go for the Rewards Card If . . . you plan to indeed pay off the balance on the card every month. While you're at it, make sure the card also has a long grace period. *Grace period*: the number of days you have to fully pay off your bill without getting slapped with a finance charge. As for the perks, decide what's more important to you—cash back or frequent-flier miles, the two most popular forms of "rewards" these days. Few cards offer both. Cards that offer cash back are especially popular since many don't require annual fees. On the flip side, cards that boast frequent-flier miles are losing their luster because the miles are getting harder to redeem. Other perks may include extended warranties on purchases or free car-rental insurance.

Ignore the Perks If . . . you expect to carry a balance on the card. Instead shop for a credit card with the lowest annual percentage rate, or APR.

Resist Offers That . . . claim you've been "preapproved" for a "0 percent" introductory APR. It doesn't always mean you will get that same offer when you apply. And what's worse, the credit line may just be for a measly $500, which seems like a waste of time and ink filling out the application. Instead, factor in future rates. Every valid credit-card solicitation should include a box that discloses all the fees and pricing terms.

Watch Out for Fees When . . . transferring debt. Shifting credit-card debt from a high-interest-rate credit card to one with a lower rate can save money, but watch out for "transfer" or "transaction" fees, which can be as hefty as 3 percent of the transferred balance. Look for a low-rate balance transfer offer of at least six months to a year. Keep in mind: Those with a good credit score (anything above 680) can usually qualify for a 0 percent transfer fee.

Don't Go Crazy If . . . you're looking to get more credit. Best to limit your number of credit cards to two. Otherwise, says my friend Greg McBride, a senior financial analyst with bankrate.com (one of my favorite sites), "there is a temptation to run up debt." It's sort of human nature—the more you "have," the more you think you can spend. Plus, remember, each time you open a credit-card account, the card company issues a credit inquiry, which can easily slash 10 percent off your credit score.

Bottom-line Rule of Thumb. Have *one* card with a low APR for big-ticket purchases, like furniture or electronics, and a *second* card for day-to-day expenditures that you pay in full each month, like gas and groceries. A debit card works well for this. If you choose to get a second credit card to pay off each month, it may be helpful to subtract the day-to-day credit-card purchases from your bank account and keep track of your new balance. (Don't let it go to zero.) This way, when you go to pay off the credit card at the end of month, you can write a check knowing there's enough money in your bank account to pay off the plastic.

Oh, And. By no means should you wait for the credit-card solicitations to come through the post. Check out deals offered at your bank, as well as on Web sites such as www. bankrate.com, www .cardweb.com, www.bankingmyway.com, and www.cardratings .com. Be proactive and maybe you can get a better rate. And, once you settle on a card or cards, call 1-888-5-OPTOUT to reduce the number of credit-card solicitations in your mailbox.

➤ ➤ ➤ ➤ **Picking Apart Prepaid Cards**

Just a little FYI on prepaid cards, which are kind of like debit cards in that you need to have actual money in them to use them. Because they're like a noncredit credit card, they may be a smart supplement, or better yet, *alternative,* to credit cards. My esteemed researcher Tim Chan did a little digging around and found out the following:

PROS

➤ Prepaid credit cards are much easier to get than standard credit cards. Just about anyone and everyone who applies for a prepaid card gets their application accepted. You can even order a prepaid credit card online from the convenience of your home.

➤ There are no credit checks or minimum income requirements.

CONS

➤ The setup or activation fee is usually around $20 and can go as high as $50. On the bright side, unlike regular credit cards, which usually charge an annual fee, this is usually a onetime charge.

➤ When using a prepaid credit card, no activity reports are made to the credit bureaus. That means transactions made using a prepaid card will not affect your credit history. This can be either an advantage or a disadvantage, depending upon your spending habits and payment history.

LOWEST ON THE TOTEM POLE: GOOD OLD COLLEGE DEBT

Now we've worked our way to the bottom of the totem pole and back to Dustin and his student loans. The feds aren't after my Nittany Lion friend for ignoring his financial obligations because during those five years he was just playing by the official rules of *forbearance.* See, shortly after graduating he met with his lender, Sallie Mae, and pled that he was in no financial shape to pay back his student debt in the immediate future. How come? Well, Dustin was moving to L.A., where he would end up making $8.50 an hour at the Beverly Center Bloomingdales selling $400 denim to Drew Barrymore. True story. By night, he'd hopefully collect $200 in tips working at Jerry's Famous Deli. (Bob Sagat, Dustin tells me, likes to come in for Jerry's famous matzo ball soup after midnight with his entourage.) What's more, Dustin already had some $5,000 in credit-card debt. To summate: Tremendous debt plus low-paying job equals one sympathetic Sallie Mae account representative. According to Dustin, the nice woman at the lending office empathized with his strapped financial situation and decided to cut him some slack by offering him a grace period of sixty months before he'd have to start his monthly repayment plan. Nice job, Dustin.

That said, D's story is unique; forbearance doesn't apply to any and all. To be more technical, forbearance applies only to borrowers in dire financial situations. You need to prove your salary is weak (or, better yet, nonexistent) and that your outstanding loans, like credit-card debt, medical bills (if applicable), and so on, run unmanageably high. It also helps if you have dependents (though not a good excuse to start having children). Under the rules of forbearance, the interest you avoid during the extended grace period piles onto the principal balance (i.e., the loan amount). Essentially, this means that once the forbearance period is over, your principal will have grown and on top of that, you'll still need to pay interest. That's the downside. The plus side: You don't have to worry about the payments for some time after graduating, which opens up your monthly cash flow temporarily. That may be a wise time to start paying off the credit-card debt.

Something to keep in mind: Just because student-loan debt sits at the bottom of the totem pole and it can be managed with some flexibility, lenders don't like it when payments aren't received on time. Delinquent payments are still a slap on the old credit score.

➤ ➤ ➤ ➤ My Big Fat College Debt and How I Didn't Let It Ruin Me

These days, debt starts piling long before the ribboned diploma's in hand. The most recent stats from the College Board say undergraduates attending a for-profit college borrowed a median $24,600 over four years. Incidentally, that's almost how much student loan debt I carried after ten months at Columbia's Graduate School of Journalism. (The advance I got for this book helped me wipe out the entire remaining loan.) Say you go to a school that's a little cheaper than Columbia: At a private, nonprofit college the median undergraduate loan is $19,500, and $15,500 at a public four-year college. That's a far shout from the average student loans of past generations, back when paying for college was a small fraction of today's room and board and when financial aid was much more accessible. This might leave you thinking, why not just skip college?! Well, most of us would be worse off financially in the long run for bailing on higher education: The most recent census research shows that, on average, a person with a bachelor's degree earns roughly $51,500 a year versus just $28,600 annually with only a high school diploma.

How I tried to curb the financial pain? I found ways to save on other expenses, namely rent. I paid just $500 a month for my own bedroom in Manhattan, which may seem like a lot if you're from anywhere *but* New York. (The average share in Manhattan on the Upper West Side where I lived at the time was anywhere from $850 to $1,300 a month.) I knew I was making out way better than anyone in my grad program since "graduate housing" at Columbia (which was more like a glorified dorm room), back then, cost roughly $800 a month. Not to mention *my* room came fully furnished. It had its own air conditioner, super-fast WiFi, a private bathroom, and lovely purple paint. The drawbacks: The apartment came decorated with a newly married couple in their late forties. (They had their own bedroom.) They also had a cat (thumbs down). Add to that drama: Anna wanted to have a baby (at age forty-eight no less). Paul wanted no kids and was desperate for a brownstone in Brooklyn with a backyard. Conclusion: Paul moved out. Anna still managed to deliver a bouncing baby girl. I discovered my next book. And all the while, I was saving a bundle on rent, which I could put toward my loans! If you're already out of college and strapped with loans, you can find similar ways to cut corners, free up some cash, and apply it toward your debt.

CONSOLE-IDATE YOUR DEBT, *BUT ONLY IF IT MAKES SENSE*

Now for some practical, universal advice for borrowers who, unlike Dustin, are not as financially strapped but still want to free up their finances and make their student loan(s) more affordable. Before Dustin left Sallie Mae, he made sure to consolidate all of his outstanding college loans. He had two different ones: Stafford and Perkins. *Consolidate translation*: Your original student loans are paid off and grouped together in a brand-new loan. The interest rate becomes fixed and your repayment period may get extended by as much as twenty years. Most borrowers have a window period of six to nine months following graduation, during which time you can avoid beginning payment on your college loan and also consolidate multiple loans. By consolidating, the overall loan becomes more expensive in the long run, but when you're twenty-two years old, your immediate cash flow is often much more critical. On average, according to Sallie Mae, consolidating your student loans can save you at least 50 percent. That may mean the difference between renting a place that's five minutes from work or living at home and commuting an hour and a half every morning and evening.

Up until a couple of years ago, consolidating your student loans was a simple *duh*-move. If you had multiple student loans, you went to your original lender before the six- or nine-month grace period and sealed a better deal. But the federal government has recently done away with the rule that forced you to consolidate with your *original* lender. Now you can shop around. This may make the process of consolidating a bit more involved, but it's ultimately a good thing because it means more choices for you—and lenders are offering different incentives to win your business. (Check out the sidebar Rate Perks on how to haggle down your rate.)

That said, consolidation isn't for everyone. Obviously if you have just one loan, consolidating doesn't apply. You may, instead, opt to refinance the loan if you discover a loan vehicle with a lower, fixed interest rate. Second, if you're someone with just a few years left on your college loan, refinancing may just end up stretching out the term of the loan and hence, you'd be stuck paying *more* interest. And if the rate on your loans is less than the consolidation rate, well, then that's just easy math. Forget about it.

➤ ➤ ➤ ➤ ➤ Rate Perks

You want to get the lowest consolidation rate possible. That means going to Uncle Sam, since the government sets the rates for consistency from lender to lender. The good news is, once you dot the *i* on your interest rate, it's solid locked. Unlike your electric bill, you never have to worry about the size of your student loan bill each month after grouping together all your loans and getting one underlying fixed rate. But you can shop around for lenders with better repayment *options* and *rewards,* which can save you money down the road.

Auto pay. Ask lenders if they offer a discount for having your monthly payments automatically transferred from a checking or savings account. Some will slash your rate by as much as a quarter percent if you pay electronically.

Be good. You can often get a reduction for being on your best behavior. If you pay on time consistently for a certain period, some lenders may knock percentage points off your interest rate for the remaining term of the loan by as much as 2 percent!

And if you've already consolidated, you can't consolidate again, unless you take on another new loan (for example, if you went back to school).

As for Dustin, consolidating his loans soon after graduating brought his monthly bill to about $100 a month. But because he is in forbearance, he will have to fork over all the interest accrued on the loan during the years he managed to avoid the loan. But the short-term freedom of not having to deal with his student loans let D pay off his $5,000 credit-card bill and roll some of his new income into a 401(k) retirement plan. And best of all, it's bought him more time to devote to his screenplay— which is still a work-in-progress.

➤ ➤ ➤ ➤ Coping with Collection Agencies

For credit-card debt, there are temporary ways to avoid the wrath of collection agencies when they come aringin'.

Know your rights. Even though you owe money, there are certain rules collectors must follow under the federal Fair Debt Collection Practices Act. You can learn more by calling the Federal Trade Commission's hotline at 1-877-FTC-HELP. Here's how collection agencies break the rules:

➤ calling you at odd hours like before 8 A.M. or after 9 P.M.
➤ calling you repeatedly
➤ calling you at work if you've told them your boss doesn't allow such calls
➤ harassing or threatening you

Take a preemptive stance. Before it gets to the stage where collection agents are tying up your phone line, as soon as you find yourself having trouble paying off your debt, contact your lender. Once they learn about your situation, lenders often help by offering deferral or interest-only payment plans. Suddenly you may have more options than just screening phone calls.

CHAPTER 3

BANKING IN BED AND SCORING

How to Be a Smooth Money Operator

When I was six, I remember going to our neighborhood drive-through bank with my parents. The concept of anything drive-through in my six-year-old head always involved the magical golden arches. So, it was always a drag, driving up at this bank, mouth watering for Chicken McNuggets, to see a visorless, nerdy teller behind a Plexiglas window. Sometimes she'd have money in a white envelope for my dad. Other times she'd take *his* money. What was this covert operation? It was awfully confusing. The teller would usually slip me a lollipop through the hole in the window. Not quite Chicken McNuggets, but who refuses free candy?

Fast-forward to the twenty-first century. The fact that drive-through banks still exist bemuses me. Why spend money on gas to make a simple bank transaction? (Sure, sure, sometimes it allows for a faster check deposit, I'll give you that.) Granted, the habit of going to an actual, physical bank is not as common today as, say, it was in 1986. Since Al Gore invented the World Wide Web, many people bank almost exclusively on the Internet. You can quickly and conveniently apply for a mortgage, pay bills, deposit money, and buy shares of Apple from your laptop. You know all this already, but there are still many—like your parents—who've yet to adopt the Internet as a place to bank, and they're way behind. They're missing out on better interest rates, a chance to boost their credit score, and the opportunity to save precious time. Going to a bank requires waiting in line and dealing with a middle person. That's *so* 1986.

That said, I must confess that up until a few years ago, I banked with an actual brick-and-mortar Washington Mutual near my old office in downtown New York City. Although it was oh-so-conveniently located just minutes away from my building, too often I'd end up wasting my entire lunch hour to make a deposit. Stupid. Truth be told, I had several other options besides standing in line. For one, I could have been more organized and transferred my money directly to my checking account. But looking back, I think I just didn't trust the whole e-banking system. I was worried my money would get "lost" or that it would take several days for the money to transfer, during which time I had to eat. I was afraid some hacker would intercept my routing number and steal the remaining $80.56 I had left in my account. I suppose that's the fear that ignites when you're twenty-three and living paycheck to paycheck. But there's no excuse for not taking advantage of online banking—no matter how big or small your paycheck.

Still, online banking isn't bulletproof. You can get screwed and your ID *can* get stolen, but banks can get robbed as well. If you do your homework you can get a lot out of the www banking system and avoid cyber pitfalls. (And oh yeah, I *know* Al Gore didn't invent the Internet.)

➤ ➤ ➤ ➤ **Automate and Liberate . . . in an Hour**

We're too busy to be bothered with writing and depositing checks. Plus, a paperless society helps the environment. In the end, everyone wins when you automate your financial life, so keep reading to learn how to set it up. Remember: If any of your primary banking information changes, if you change banks or close checking accounts or if your credit card expires, you need to update affected online accounts to reflect the new routing and account numbers. And if it helps, make a note of any regular direct payments/deposits on a calendar either on your computer, on your fridge, or in your BlackBerry. Just because your ATM receipt says you've got $500 left in checking, Verizon may go into your account in the next day or two to deduct the amount you owe for the month. Don't hit H&M just yet.

Your paycheck. Contact HR. Tell them you want to get your paycheck deposited directly into your checking or savings account. You'll need your bank's information, including the routing number for your account. My favorite thing about this is that direct deposit usually means I get my money a day or two in advance of the scheduled payday. My credit union tells me this is because some employers let banks know up to a couple of days beforehand how much money will go into the account on payday. Most banks will credit your account as soon as they find out, as a courtesy. It's not a float; the money's yours to draw early.

HBO and cell. Your cable and telephone bills (both cellular and land-line) can usually get taken care of electronically through each respective company's Web site. There, you can open an online account, enter your banking information, and presto—your next bill will automatically get deducted.

Bloomingdale's and heat. Mycheckfree.com is where I manage my bills for everything from my Bloomingdale's account to my electricity and gas bills.

Note: Sometimes it costs *more* to pay online. The 50¢ you save on stamps may seem like nothing compared to the extra dollars some places charge as a "convenience fee" to pay online. For example, the City of New York charges me an extra $15 for paying my property taxes online.

PICKING A CYBER BANK

I already feel guilty for using the word *homework*. I see that word all the time in financial how-to books, without any practical, qualifying instructions. Closed-end messages like "Avoid cyber theft: Do your homework," or "Avoid bankruptcy: Do your homework." Thanks, but what is in the lesson plan, exactly? So here's my assignment for what to look for in a cyber bank that will keep your money safe and growing.

1. Dual Presence

Narrow down online banks to those that have a nearby physical location, too, with human employees who can help you in case of an emergency. It sometimes beats waiting on the phone for a customer-service rep. And in some cases, face-to-face interaction still works best.

Online banks with no physical location, like www.ingdirect .com, www.everdirect.com, and www.univest.net, have their advantages as well, but they don't really serve as a *sole* place to stash your money. They're great supplementary *savings* banks. They're starting to offer high-yield checking accounts, too, but I'll dive into the pros and cons later in this chapter.

2. Check in with Credit Unions

Since I was seventeen, I've had the same savings and checking accounts with the Digital Credit Union, or www.dcu.org, in Massachusetts. Sounds kind of dorky—credit union. How and why am I choosing such an unfashionable bank? Well, my dad used to work for a division within Digital Equipment Corporation, which had an affiliated credit union offering perks like fee-free checking and competitive interest rates for employees and their families. Generally speaking, credit unions are not-for-profit institutions, so they don't have to subject their banking clients to exorbitant fees, like for-profit banks do. And you don't necessarily have to be an employee or member of an organization to join a credit union. Being a tax-paying member of the community usually suffices. The one caveat to credit unions is they typically have fewer physical branches and ATMs than major bank networks. And now that I live in New York City, it's impossible to visit a DCU branch. But I haven't needed a reason to go inside one during the past ten years. Instead, if I have problems or concerns, I can get to a phone rep on the spot. The customer-service line is much faster than a larger financial institution's would be. The bank's online presence is crucial, and, frankly, I wouldn't be a member if it didn't have online checking capabilities. At www.dcu.org I can transfer money to either my checking, savings, or credit-card account. I can also schedule payments to my mortgage lender and, of course, check my balances. And back before I direct deposited my paychecks, I used to mail in my checks with DCU's stamp-free deposit slips, which was pretty nice. The only downside was my money would usually get deposited some five days later. But now I can freely route my checks directly to DCU. To find a credit union near you, go to www.creditunion.coop.

3. Free Checking?

If a credit union isn't convenient or sexy enough, begin your search for an online commercial bank that offers "free checking." (Note: The USAA Federal Savings Bank has opened its banking services to the public and offers a free checking account and free checks. Visit usaa.com.) Often *free checking* means you are not forced to keep a minimum balance in your account and can write as many checks a month as you like. Just because you don't see *free checking* doesn't mean it doesn't exist. This isn't exactly a perk banks boldly advertise, so call up and speak with a rep to verify.

4. What Are the Fees, Please?

Banks make most of their money from fees generated from you and me. Yep, that's right. That's why we need to be extra vigilant, read the fine print, and ask human reps what sort of damage bill an average client can expect. What if I use another bank's ATMs? What if I bounce a check? What if I close my account? What if I don't feel like putting a lot of money into my savings account right now? Likely answers: Fee. Fee. Fee. And fee. But there are banks with fewer penalties for such things and that's where the homework pays off. Both www.bankrate.com and www.bankingmyway.com will even do some of it for you—go to either site to compare fees for all the major banks both online and in brick and mortar.

5. How Fast Will My Money Grow?

In other words: What's the annual percent yield (APY) or interest rate on my checking and savings accounts? While some savings accounts can fetch as high as 5 percent annually, checking accounts earn relatively *little* interest at traditional online banks. In fact, the average APY for checking accounts with balances of $5,000 or more is only 0.36 percent, according to Informa Research Services. In some cases, then, it may be worth having a savings account at one bank and a checking account somewhere else. More and more, online banks are offering higher APY checking accounts to woo us. But watch out; find out the minimum opening balance requirement, which may range anywhere from $1 to $2,500. Also, some banks, including the virtual ones, may charge a fee or offer *less* interest every time the monthly balance falls below the minimum requirement. At E*Trade, for example, the minimum balance of

$5,000 receives a competitive 3.6 percent yield, but balances less than $5,000 earn just 0.5 percent.

➤ ➤ ➤ ➤ ➤ One Serving of Overdraft Protection, Please

Overdraft protection rocks, especially since "insufficient-fund" fees average close to $30 a bounce. And who wants a $30 hole in his or her wallet? In college I would have been at least $100 richer one semester had I just opted for overdraft protection. I had no idea a series of checks I'd written would all get withdrawn at the same time! Plus my most recent ATM receipt said I had money—when I really didn't. The argument sort of worked on the phone with the customer-service representative. He got rid of half the insufficient-fund charges. But that wasn't lesson learned for me. I still bounced checks the next semester. It wasn't until I got in the habit of regularly checking my account *online* to see what still hadn't cleared and also signed up for overdraft protection that I completely kicked this very stupid and expensive habit. With overdraft protection, the bank generally links your checking and savings accounts to cover each other's butts in the event of insufficient funds in one account. It costs, on average, about $3 a month. Absolutely choose a bank that offers this.

➤ ➤ ➤ ➤ ➤ Give the ATM Attitude

ATMs should give you money, not eat it! Choose a bank with many of its own ATM locations nearby to avoid your bank's "foreign-withdrawal" fees, which can be anywhere from $1 to $3 per transaction. Know where to find the surcharge-free ATMs, too, since those can be another $2.50 per transaction. The Independent Community Bankers of America offers a searchable list of more than a thousand free ATMs at icba.org. You can avoid the ATM altogether by going to stores offering "cash back" when you use your ATM card for purchases. How it works: You ring up stuff. It can be as small a purchase as a pack of Juicy Fruit. You use your debit card to pay for said stuff. The clerk or PIN machine asks you if you want "cash back," which means do you want some cash from your debit card at no additional charge or fee? You say yes. You beat the system.

Here's a list of stores I found nationwide with this service. In most cases there's a smaller limit to how much you can withdraw, usually $20 to $60.

Tower Records (whichever ones are left)

Gristedes

Associated Supermarkets

Staples

Rite-Aid

Walgreens

Whole Foods

Best Buy

Circuit City

SCORE. BIG-TIME.

Beyond standardized test scores that tend to haunt us through academia (I am still too embarrassed to admit my first round of SAT scores), there's the almighty CREDIT score. Dahn dahn dahn. It is a critical number, assigned to us as early as the day we open our first credit-card or savings account. It's also extremely judgmental, ranking our worthiness as borrowers, employees, sometimes even spouses (just ask the percentage of today's divorcees who split over financial constraints). If you want *real* assets like a car and a home, you have to keep score. In essence, this number, which ranges from 300 to 850 can be the key to living life to its financial fullest (although almost no one scores 850—700 or better is considered Ivy

League grade). If your score is lower than 700, there are ways to boost it to ensure that you not only qualify for a loan, but that you snag the lowest possible interest rate.

Regardless of your score, you should regularly monitor your credit activity. The Federal Trade Commission lets us get a copy of our credit report from each of the three major credit-reporting agencies each year, which you can do by visiting www.annualcreditreport .com, the only authorized site to obtain your free credit reports. You can also call 1-877-322-8228 to order them. This report will include very important summaries of your credit record to which lenders and employers have access: your credit activity, your payment and default histories, etc. But the credit report doesn't give you your actual credit *score*. That you will have to buy from one of the credit reporting agencies directly: www.experian.com, www.equifax.com, or www.transunion.com. Know that if your credit report is problematic, your credit score will likely be affected, too. (Note: It is best to stagger the offers for a free credit report from each of the agencies and get three reports *throughout* the year. This not only helps you stay on top of your credit report and score but also helps you monitor your accounts frequently for signs of ID theft.)

➤ ➤ ➤ ➤ ➤ **Alternative Testing 101**

The country's big three credit-reporting agencies have recently joined forces to create a new credit-scoring model called VantageScore. It intends to rival the traditional FICO (Fair Isaac Corp.) credit-scoring system, which uses a scale of 300 to 850.

VantageScore, meantime, uses a scale of 501 to 990 and correlates the score to a grade. This system is not as widely used as FICO, and when I refer to numeric credit scores in this book, I'm following FICO's scale, not VantageScore's.

The VantageScore scale looks like this:

901 to 990 equals "A" credit

801 to 900 equals "B" credit

701 to 800 equals "C" credit

601 to 700 equals "D" credit

501 to 600 equals "F" credit

FEED ME—NOURISHING YOUR SCORE

Like credit-card debt, a credit score is intangible, which leads some of us to think it's not *really* there, that it doesn't quite exist. After all, we're not in the habit of checking this number as incessantly as, say, scores on espn.com or our weight on the scale. But even though it's not in our face, how we manage our daily finances affects this almighty triple-digit score. Here's how we can boost it.

Be on Time. The first key to raising your credit score is (duh) paying your bills on time. Falling behind on your monthly student loan or failing to pay your cable bill can knock down the score by 10 or more points. It happens to the best of us, even those of us without ADD. Automatic payments can help. More on that in the next chapter.

Get the Ratio Right. Your credit score is also based on what's called the debt-to-available-credit ratio. In other words, how much you owe versus your credit allowance. If you have a $10,000 limit on your Visa and you owe $8,000, that's way too high. As I've mentioned, best to keep your credit ratio to below 30 percent lest your credit score takes a direct hit.

Know That Time Heals. Time can also work on your side. If you've been bad with debt in the past, know that *recent* events can have more impact on your score than previous missteps. Be good.

THAT'S GONNA LEAVE A MARK—*CREDIT SCORE MISSTEPS*

Applying for More Credit. Each time you apply for a credit card, whether through one of the big credit lenders like Visa, Master-Card, American Express, and so on, or at a store, the lender issues an inquiry on your credit history. The act of "inquiring" doesn't look too hot on your records—even though you've done nothing wrong.

Closing Accounts. If you have a credit card you opened in college and you've successfully paid it off, (1) bravo, and (2) don't close the account. Why? Isn't a closed account better than an open one? Not necessarily. Keeping the account open will boost the denominator in that debt-to-available-credit ratio. Best advice: Pay off the card. Keep it open. Just don't use it again. So you're not tempted, throw it away but don't tell anyone, especially Visa, MasterCard, or the Gap. Sometimes, though, store credit cards break up with you for lack of attention. Not too long ago, I got a letter from Pier 1 Imports saying "due to the inactivity on your card, we're closing your account" (yet another reason it's so hard to win with store credit cards). But my friend Lisa gave me great advice for the next time I decide to stop using a card. A financial adviser told her she should write letters to the banks or stores that issued the credit cards saying: "After reviewing my finances, I have decided that I do not need the credit card at this time." The key phrase there is "at this time" so the banks and stores are under the impression you might be a client again in the future, which makes them less likely to close your account. Keep copies of those letters, too.

➤ ➤ ➤ ➤ Reclaim Your Credit Reputation . . . in an Hour

Credit-reporting agencies aren't always right. They could have erroneous payment histories, the wrong date of birth, or have you listed as dead (it's happened). Here's how to fight back.

Discover it. Sounds obvious, but if you don't check your credit report at least once annually, you're in the dark.

Probe it. Ask for an investigation by filing a dispute online at one or more of the credit-reporting bureaus that's showing the error: www .experian.com, www.equifax.com, or www.transunion.com. Include your full name, home address, birth date, and Social Security number. Mention the company you believe made the mistake and the account number. Explain the problem and how it can be corrected.

Trace it. To the best of your ability, gather your own evidence as backup to prove the mistake is, indeed, a mistake. For example, find receipts if it's a payment dispute. If it was a cashed check, your bank should have a record. If it was a credit-card-payment error, check with your card's issuer.

Wait for it. It takes about forty to sixty days, beginning to end, to dispute a mistake. You, as the rightfully angry client, have thirty days for the lender to respond and provide documentation. If they fail, then the dispute is automatically resolved in your favor, the deserved consumer. Your credit report should be fixed and accurate within sixty days.

CHAPTER 4

RICH PEOPLE DRESS GOOD

Being a Smart Consumer Pays

One of my favorite finance profs at Penn State, Tim Simin, used to remind his students as we headed out the door before a final exam that "rich people dress good!!" His grammatically incorrect and unfactual rallying cry said that if we memorized the formula for CapM (Capital Asset Pricing Model), we'd ace the test, get an A in the class, graduate with honors, land a job at Goldman Sachs, and, voilà, be able to afford all of life's luxuries, including Gucci sunglasses and whatever else rich people buy to make themselves feel rich.

The average grade on the final was a C–. Did that mean more than half of us would be stuck wearing Old Navy for the rest of our lives? Sorry, but I don't do performance fleece.

Even if you don't work at Goldman Sachs or make enough money to be a rich person, you can still dress rich. Trust me, I've devised strategies to avoid burning a whole through my wallet when I go to Nordstrom. (And P.S. Even with less money, you and I both know we can dress better than most of the "rich" folk out there. After all, having money doesn't always mean having taste.)

THERE'S NO SAFETY IN NUMBERS

One of the worst days of my first summer in New York was the kickoff to the Bloomingdale's summer sale. I was a lowly intern and could only escape to the department store during my lunch hour under the guise of "going to the dentist."

Dashing to the second floor, I immediately spotted what I wanted. Correction: needed. The dark-wash designer jeans that I had been eyeing since May were now about 30 percent off. But by the time I got to the store, the only ones left were in sizes fit for Nicole Richie (postrehab, prepregnancy). I learned my lesson quickly and painfully: I needed to stop eating.

But the real, practical lesson was that I should've bought the jeans at the *regular* price back in May—meaning I would've had to assess my hierarchy of need-wants. After all, being a smart shopper doesn't mean exclusively buying items on sale. The most-worn items in my closet (and the most cared for items, I might add) are my $300 Paige white denim jeans, my $195 Michael Kors sandals, and my Fendi purse (a hand-me-down from my mom, sort of. She thinks I'm just borrowing it).

On the other hand, my $8 H&M cotton T-shirt always shrinks or discolors in the wash and I can't seem to find those TJ Maxx sunglasses . . . oh well, they were just $9.99. But those little purchases—no matter how small they seem at the time—add up. Which is to say, there's no safety in numbers when it comes to shopping. I used to go through four or five pairs of Chinatown shades a year, each either left on a city bus or broken after a week. Why? Because, I guess, psychologically it was no big whoop to misplace or break something that was "made in China" for 13¢ and sold here for $5. But over the course of a few years, I probably spent as much on plastic sunglasses that did little to protect me

from UV rays as I finally did on a sweet pair of Ray-Bans purchased once and lasting a lifetime.

Bottom Line. Sometimes you're better off going for the splurge,
but *only* the splurge and only when it makes sense. Spending an
arm and a leg on fancy hair products or organic food is sometimes
a waste of money. For more on what's worth splurging for and
what's not, see the Should I Splurge? sidebar.

BEFORE YOU HIT THE REGISTER

Tim Chan, my twenty-five-year-old research assistant and barom-
eter of coolness, always asks himself this before buying an item on
sale: "Would I buy it if it *wasn't* on the sale rack?" Because, he admits, while that orange cashmere sweater from Barney's is pretty
inexpensive at $15, it's also orange and, hello, a turtleneck—*gross!*
When are you ever going to wear that besides maybe Halloween
and Queens Day in Amsterdam?

Instead, choose a color that's likely to match the rest of your
wardrobe. Chances are spending $100 on a black cashmere sweater
is more of an investment than orange or lime green. You buy it
once, it goes with everything, and you wear it always.

Also, Sam Saboura, the style host of ABC's *Extreme Make-
over,* and someone I refer to for fashion-buying tips, suggests
doing what's called the walk-around. If you see something you
like in a store and are afraid of buying on impulse, put it aside at
the register and take a walk around the mall or the block. If you
come back and are *still* convinced the orange turtleneck sweater
will make you a happier person and you will wear it more than
once a month (even in the summer), go for it. Then, walk
quickly past the new fall items. Think of it like being on the
Atkins diet. Full-price items are protein. Sale items are carbs. If

you overdose on carbs, the diet doesn't work and you get fatter. You need to be selective and smart about what you put in your mouth (and closet, as it is).

➤ ➤ ➤ ➤ Should I Splurge?

A lot of times it comes down to technicals and whether a certain product offers more value (i.e., makes you hotter or healthier or both).

Sure it's great to have a bathroom full of Kiehl's products, but not when they cost you a fortune and not when the CVS-brand stuff can be just as effective. Here's a list of things you should be paying good money for and things that you can save on without tarnishing your radiance.

Skin moisturizer? Save. Most drugstore-brand moisturizers provide good hydration and work for men and women of all skin types. Many now also include an SPF to protect your skin from sun damage.

Cleansers? Save. Cleansers are meant to do exactly that—cleanse. You don't want a product that's meant to strip away all the impurities on your face to have a lot of ingredients that will actually *add* stuff. Many expensive cleansers have fragrances and medical ingredients that can actually irritate the skin. It's better to look for something simpler. (If you suffer from acne, it's a different story. See what your dermatologist recommends.)

Eye shadow? Splurge. Department-store eye shadows, like Clinique and Nars, usually have richer colors and stay on longer. Since they are more finely milled than drugstore brands, like Maybelline and Cover Girl, they are also less likely to clump or crumble. Some colors are more expensive to make than others, due to their pigmentation, and drugstores are usually limited to browns and blues. If you want a more exotic color, you're better off going for the splurge.

Foundation? Splurge. It's important to find the right shade of foundation to match your skin tone, and cheaper brands usually have only a few generic hues. You don't want to settle on the cheap foundation and end up looking orange or any other shade of unnatural. Department-store foundations also apply more evenly and are less likely to rub off. You can wear that white blouse with confidence!

Blush? Splurge. Similar to foundations, it's important to find a shade of blush that will compliment your skin tone. Cheaper powder blushes have been diluted with talcum powder and are not as rich in color. Some may also leave streaks, if they have not been diluted smoothly.

Mascara? Save. According to experts, drugstore-brand mascaras actually outsell those found in department stores. The reason? You don't need a lot of mascara to get the effect you want and most color formulas are the same. (It's very difficult to mess up black.) The trick is to get a good mascara brush that will let you apply it evenly, without clumping.

Eyeliner? Depends. If you're going to be poking something so close to your eye, make sure it is well made and easy to apply. Drugstore eyeliners tend to break and many of them are so hard that they irritate the eye. Spend your money on eyeliner with a soft tip that goes on smoothly. But then my editor swears by her $6 Cover Girl eyeliner, a savings of $12 compared to the Clinque brand she used to wear. Whatever works, I guess.

Shampoo? Save. Shampoos are meant to cleanse your hair; despite all the formulas with vitamins and proteins, the fact remains that your hair really doesn't absorb much of it. Consider this: Most regular shampoos will give you the same effect as "volumizing" shampoos. What gives your hair volume and the "bouncy" feeling is not a secret formula, but rather cleansing it of dirty buildup and impurities. Any shampoo will do that.

Conditioner? Splurge. The type of conditioner needed varies according to hair type so it's not a good idea to buy a generic formula. Someone with coarse hair needs different conditioning than someone with thick, wavy hair. While shampoos often rinse out when you wash your hair, many ingredients found in conditioners stay (things like oil and wax, which leave your hair with that great shine).

Styling products? Depends. Like conditioner, different hair textures require different products. Sometimes a generic gel won't do for your 'do. So invest in a grooming aid that is right for your hair type and the hair style that you want. (A two-in-one tip for controlling frizzies in humid weather: hand-moisturizing lotion. This works as a great hair relaxer.)

The exception: Hair spray. It's just meant to lock in a style and any cheap bottle will do the trick.

BUTTER UP

Sometimes it pays to warm up to the sales staff, who will whisper advance notice of sales and coupons if they like you. Sales associates also have access to "Friends and Family" coupons, which, in some cases, offer discounts of up to 30 percent. If you're at a small store spending more than $100, simply *ask* for a discount. That's right: Ask. Say you really like the store and plan on returning. It sounds strange, but you'll usually shave 10 percent or more off the price tag—in some cities that's like avoiding sales tax. Sam once told me he saved 30 percent on a $400 piece of luggage at a small boutique just by asking if there was a sale and whether he could get a discount. The saleslady responded with a "No . . . but we're having a sale next week" . . . pause . . . "but, I can give you an *advance* discount (wink)." And no, it wasn't because she recognized him from TV. Sam was just that overly sweet customer who made her feel special.

DRESS FOR THE JOB YOU WANT, NOT THE JOB YOU HAVE

We all want to make more money and that usually means climbing the ladder at work. If I learned anything from being in the corporate world, it's that how you dress matters at the office; if you dress like you work in the mail room, more likely than not, your coworker who's wearing a crisp button-down shirt and tie every day will be the one considered for a promotion more readily. At the least, he'll look more aware and knowledgeable. That said, I'm not suggesting you run out and slap down your credit card for a Fendi purse just because your forty-year-old six-figure-salary boss has one. Be smart about it and, most of all, *wear your confidence.* It's free!

> **Fashion $ense**
>
> A recent Yahoo/HotJobs survey found that fashion matters in the workplace. The poll discovered that a majority of the average U.S. workforce (68 percent) and HR employees (82 percent) believe appearance can affect getting promoted.

Case in Point. Amy was, in my opinion, the best dresser at *Money Magazine*, as far as I could judge during my reporting days there. She always had something interesting on and was always dressed one season ahead. But she wasn't going to trunk shows in Milan or making heaps of money as a research assistant that allowed her to shop on Madison Avenue during her lunch breaks. After a couple of drinks with her at a Midtown bar one day, I discovered the secret (and surprise) to her shopping.

Amy avoided department stores and retail chains. She went to fashion bazaars on the weekends where budding designers would show off their newest handbags, shoes, and miniskirts. In New York, fashion marketplaces can be found scattered inside churches, high school gymnasiums, and alongside piers. Prices there are always negotiable, and the best part is, you walk out with something unique and handmade by someone who may be the next Kate Spade or Ralph Lauren.

Amy was promoted three times in two years. In addition to her hard work ethic, great stories, and friendly persona, I credit part of her success to being an office standout whose outfits, shoes, and earrings let people know she was an independent thinker who didn't cry mercy to Louis Vuitton. She appeared confident, and everyone, including her boss, believed it.

Incidentally, Amy also never wore strong perfumes or crazy-colored, caked-on makeup. I think that's worth mentioning.

ONLINE SHOP

Okay. So you don't do budding-designer handbags at flea markets. . . . Still vying for the Coach tote? The Internet is a vast savings vehicle for shopping. EBay is always my first stop. And remember, just because you're saving 20 percent on a designer bag by buying it online, it's *still* a splurge. Make sure it's worth your wallet. Promise you won't be at Marshall's next month scooping up three discounted bags. Do as the French do and be selective. Seriously, that's why they don't get fat.

Not only do most sites offer free shipping, but several Web sites do the comparison shopping for you. Here are a few popular price-comparison sites: www.shopping.com, www.bizrate.com, www.mysimon.com, and www.pricegrabber.com.

There are also Web sites, like www.overstock.com, that sell name-brand overproduced and discontinued items.

Finally, sites like www.net-a-porter.com, www.revolveclothing

.com, and www.bluefly.com offer designer clothing and accessories on sale.

> **E-shopping Discoveries**
>
> The site www.bluefly.com, a popular designer discount retailer, updates with new merchandise at 6:30 A.M., and www.overstock.com has some exceptional deals on comforters every day.

➤ ➤ ➤ ➤ ➤ **How Aaliyah Dresses Good**

You'll see Aaliyah again in chapter 10. Her life is just too good! Here's how she manages how to have such a fabulous wardrobe.

Her freebies. Though she's not getting paid at her fashion magazine internship, she's bagged a lot of goodies from the sample rack in the office. When the fashion editor scoffed at last fall's taupe silk scarf, she offered it to Aaliyah, who gladly took it to complete her Friday-evening wardrobe. When the book editor threw out a bunch of computer guides, Aaliyah scooped them up and sold them at a used bookstore for ten bucks each (which then paid for a new pair of jeans). A leftover bracelet from the jewelry department became a wedding gift for her cousin (shh). Meantime, Aaliyah is helping the fashion designer build her Web site for free. But in return she gets free clothes that are one-of-a-kind samples that would normally retail in the hundreds. "It's better than buying the same blouse that everyone else has from H&M," she says.

Her money mantra. "Saving money is not easy and I hate having to put aside a certain amount each week as 'untouchable money.' It's so old-fashioned. I practice 'selective saving.' On weeks where I'm eyeing a certain pair of sneakers or want to go for a manicure, I'll put aside 10 percent of my tips and paycheck. Then at the end of the week, I use what I've saved to purchase that desired product. Saving money to me makes more sense when you have something you're saving toward."

➤ ➤ ➤ ➤ How Zachary Dresses Good

Who's Zachary? Zach is twenty-seven years old, a UPenn graduate, and an international man of mystery. Seriously, he works as the executive assistant to one of the Middle East's wealthiest entrepreneurs. He's never in the same country for long. His usual destinations include Kuwait City, Lebanon, Hong Kong, London, and New York. He gets to see the world, literally, but he basically works nonstop and has limited time for romantic relationships. He wishes to be rich enough someday "to be able to provide for my family (siblings and parents included)."

His freebies. "You mean aside from the helicopter and private jet rides, the summers on the eighty-meter yacht, and the wings in mansions in exotic locations?" *Yes, Zach, aside from all that, you show-off.* "I've gotten weird freebies, depending on when and where I am. If I'm by myself, I'm essentially the voice of Oz and can tell anyone in my boss's empire to do anything for me." *Like what, Zach?* "Go out and get me sneakers, have a bar made up at my friend's rooftop for a party we're throwing, bring me my weight in fat-free yogurt." *Okay, seriously?* "Okay, seriously, some advice I have is always ask for a discount. Americans don't do this because it's embarrassing, but it's normal everywhere else in the world! Just ask, that's all. And if they're hesitant, it means that maybe they can. Most managers have authority to discount stuff by five to fifteen percent. Point out irregularities in the clothes and ask for a discount as a result." *Okay. That's better. Thanks!*

And one bit of travel advice. Buy two empty suitcases and a round-trip ticket to Beijing, shop like crazy for four days, and save hundreds.

➤ ➤ ➤ ➤ ➤ **How Kat Dresses Good**

Who is Kat? At twenty-eight years old, Kat is a producer for a major news network. She's originally from Orange County, California, likes Ketel One, getting out of the country as often as possible, and laughing.

Her shopping mantra. "I only shop with cash. It's parental advice. I take out a limited amount and that's what I can spend, though rarely do, since cash is harder to let go of."

Her favorite Web sites. "I like www.dailycandy.com and www.luckymag .com."

Tip for special-occasion outfits. Since it's just for one occasion, don't go overboard. What does she do? "Go shopping in a friend's closet!"

She would never "buy 'outfits,' because it's difficult to do. Separates can get more mileage. I think the best way to save money on clothes is to try on, for example, a shirt with some jeans in the store that are similar to your own at home. Also, see if the shirt works with a skirt or slacks. Treat the mall like your closet. You'll be less likely to splurge if you spend some time in a top and try out looks that maybe don't work."

And never, ever "go shopping if you haven't gone through your entire closet's worth of clothes," she says. Reach exhaustion!

GET YOUR MONEY BACK AND THEN SOME

We've all gotten raw deals—the dry cleaner shrunk your cashmere sweater, your steak was overcooked, the flowers you sent Grandma were wilted. You didn't get your money's worth, and sometimes because you appear young, people think they can rip you off.

But there is a way to get revenge, which takes a combo of panache and strategy. Take it from someone who grew up with immigrant parents who always suspected they were being under-estimated. You gotta prove who's right!

1. Act Fast and in Person

A nasty letter or e-mail usually gets ignored, and it can take for-ever to reach the right person by phone. The face-to-face complaint usually works best because you're not as easy to get rid of.

2. Shoot for the Top

Keep going up the chain of command until you reach someone who is helpful. If it's a franchise or a branch and the head manager is being stubborn, make it clear that you will contact headquarters and file a complaint. Some companies have "quality control" or "quality management" units that step in when customer service goes awry.

If no one at the company or store will help, mention that you're going straight to the watchdogs, like the Better Business Bureau or the attorney general's office, to file a complaint.

Case in Point. Carla Hernandez, an executive assistant at NY1 News, my old broadcast station in New York, once found a hair in her hot wings at Applebee's. Dee-lish. When the manager on duty refused to throw out her bill, she wrote a letter to the restau-rant's corporate headquarters and CC'd the city health department as well as the state attorney general. Within two days she received an apology letter from the regional sales manager and a $50 gift certificate.

3. Put on a Smile (a Fake One Works, Too)

People hate being yelled at—especially when they're not the ones who overcharged your phone bill or forgot to heat your soup, for example. Instead, express your unhappiness in a calm voice, says Lynette Padwa, author of *Say the Magic Words: How to Get What You Want from the People Who Have What You Need.* "There may be a time later for anger," Padwa says, "but don't start out that way."

Also, don't make false claims or exaggerate how much you deserve to be compensated. In other words, if your dinner arrived cold and you don't want to pay for your meal, save the drama; don't say the waiter spit on your food and spilled red wine on your new shirt.

➤ ➤ ➤ ➤ ➤ **The Art of Complaining**

Some common unpleasantries and what you should expect after nicely, honestly, and quickly complaining.

Problem: You're not satisfied with your hotel room.

Solution: Go to the reception desk and explain the problem. You can probably ask to be moved to another room or ask for a voucher for a free night at a later date.

Problem: You get a disaster haircut or coloring.

Solution: Fight back the tears and say your cut didn't turn out as you expected. Suggest how to change it. Experts say hair stylists will and should fix it for free.

Problem: Flowers you ordered for a special occasion arrive a day late.

Solution: Contact the florist and explain that unless they fix the problem, your steady won't stop crying because she thinks you forgot her birthday. In this case, it's okay to get a little dramatic. A proper florist should remedy the situation with a new bouquet and an apology letter to the recipient.

Problem: Your time was wasted while placing an order or dealing with customer service over the phone. Time is money, after all.

Solution: Ask for something in return. Usually they won't give you money but maybe merchandise. A friend once received a free digital camera from Dell after a technician took too long trying to help solve his computer problem over the phone.

EXPERT-RECOMMENDED ORGANIC BUYS

When it comes to produce, Consumer Reports says go organic on apples, bell peppers, celery, cherries, imported grapes, nectarines, peaches, pears, potatoes, red raspberries, spinach, and strawberries. Tests show these products tend to have the most pesticide residues when grown conventionally.

Meat, poultry, eggs, and dairy are other good organic buys. Organic animal-food products reduce exposure to pesticides, hormones, and antibiotics consumed by the animals in their feed.

No-Need Organic

Consumer Reports says there is less reason for buying organic versions of these products: asparagus, avocados, bananas, broccoli, cauliflower, sweet corn, kiwi, mangos, onions, papaya, pineapples, and green peas. Why? There are few residues found on these products, even when they are not organic. As a general rule of thumb, anything grown with a thick, nonedible skin or peel is A-OK.

You can also forget about the extra splurge for organic breads, oils, potato chips, pasta, cereals, and other packaged foods, such as canned or dried fruit and vegetables. Why? These foods are often highly processed anyway and may not be 100 percent organic. Read the labels carefully.

Organic seafood is another one to skip. Why? Organic standards for seafood are sometimes poor and allow contaminants or suspect ingredients. When it comes to buying shrimp, crabmeat, or salmon, you're better off worrying about freshness.

> Speaking of organic, food in this category can cost more than double the price of conventional foods, so if having an organic menu is part of your "good life," know these facts before shopping at Whole Foods and the rest.

➤ ➤ ➤ ➤ ➤ Learning Labels . . . in Five Minutes

- ➤ "100% Organic": Product must contain 100 percent organic ingredients.
- ➤ "Organic": At least 95 percent of ingredients are produced organically.
- ➤ "Made with Organic Ingredients": At least 70 percent of ingredients are organic. The remaining 30 percent must come from the USDA's approved list.
- ➤ "Free-range" or "Free-roaming": This misleading term is applied to eggs and chicken and other meat. The being did not necessarily spend a good portion of its life outdoors. The rule states only that outdoor access be available to the fowl or livestock for "an undetermined period each day." U.S. government standards are weak in this area.
- ➤ "Natural" or "All Natural": Does *not* mean organic. There is no

standard definition for this term except with meat and poultry products. (The USDA defines *natural* as not containing any artificial flavoring, colors, chemical preservatives, or synthetic ingredients.) The claim is not verified. The producer or manufacturer alone decides whether to use the term natural.

TO MARKET, TO MARKET

Make it a worthwhile trip.

Here's what's in my fridge as I type: five slices of wheat bread, some Philly cream cheese, a half-bottle of rosé wine, an array of salad dressings, a Brita water pitcher, and a ton of Smuckers. In my freezer: ice, Fudgesicles, frozen asparagus, eye mask. Yum. It's more frightening than anything else, actually. Not because I have zero food in my house (unless I want a PBJ-and-asparagus sandwich), but because my mom is most def going to call me after reading this. She'll be yelling in Farsi about how I need to stock up on *real, fresh* food. She'll ask why I have no fruit and no vegetables. She'll question my weight, ask if I'm eating enough, and then proceed to e-mail me impossible recipes for Persian meals. In another week I suspect I will also receive a giant rice cooker and a few bottles of saffron imported from Shiraz. Seriously.

But the reality is, even if I had the latest-edition rice cooker and a fridge full of organic food, I'm not home enough or interested enough when I *get* home to physically cook a meal. The thought of having to not only *wait* for food, but to also do work in order to eat it is simply torturous. If I have to boil or marinade or "let simmer," I'm useless. If I can nuke it, we can negotiate, but even then it's hard to find delicious *microwavable* foods. And I've tried the grocery thing. I've even shopped for food at www .freshdirect.com, our local online grocer that delivers to your doorstep the day after you place an order. I still can't win with that invention, either. All perishable items end up turning a fuzzy blue, which equals money down the toilet. (Consequently, this is also why I now store bread in my fridge.)

But trust me, I eat. Sometimes, way too much. I love my morning coffee from Ali Hash who runs the Good Morning America coffee cart on Wall Street. For lunch I enjoy grilled chicken salad or a turkey sandwich from the Variety Deli on Broadway. Sometimes dinner is sushi from Haru in my neighborhood or quesadillas from Café Frida (also in my nabe), and snacks include all things Kashi. Basically, I love all ready-to-eat food—food that just shows up, no stirring, sautéing, or patience required.

Hey, I'm not perfect.

However, if I had it in me to prepare my food with items from a (gasp!) grocery store, here are some tips the money-maven in me knows can help save money at the market.

Plan. Type-A personalities unite! This is a great opportunity to think ahead and make lists. Before you hit the grocery store, create a meal plan. List foods you will definitely consume at home. If you have three business dinners and a date coming up in the next week, you're not likely to eat from your fridge. Know your schedule and what you want to have in the house if you'll be eating at home.

Stretch. Spread out your shopping. We tend to overbuy if we shop once a month or once a week. Instead, make a couple of trips each week. Remember to check expiration dates and never grocery shop on an empty stomach!

Bulk Up. This works best with nonperishables—just make sure you have enough shelf space! Examples are dried beans, rice, pasta, canned goods, cereal, and spices. For singles, it may actually be cost-efficient to buy smaller items that are priced more per ounce, because they're less likely to go to waste.

As for perishable items, remember you can always seal and freeze meat and veggies for later. Consider investing in a vacuum sealer to store foods in the freezer long term.

Shop Fair. Don't pooh-pooh generics. The quality of store brands is much better than it has been in the past, and the savings can be significant—often more than 50 percent.

CHAPTER 5

ACCESSORIZE RIGHT

Guilt-Free Gadgetry (and Gym Plans, Too!)

Ever see someone listening to an old portable CD player? Or sorry, *Disc*man. Brushing the dust off his compact disc or CD to change songs? It's so sad. If the iPod was too expensive, why not get a mini MP3 player from Wal-Mart? (I just checked www .walmart.com and found one for $35.) And what are those alien headphones? Is that *foam* around the earpiece? Wow.

P.S. Tower Records just called. They want to thank you for still shopping there.

Having the latest and most stylish gadget wear, from handheld music devices to cell phones, and other electronic gizmos, may be imperative to your good life, or at least to avoid getting mocked in a personal finance book. Those of you who skipped chapters 1 through 4 and landed here first know who you are. And, indeed, these nice, pretty things cost money. I'm not insisting that Mr. Discman go out and charge $300 on his credit card for an iPod. After all, he may not need-want a fancy music player. Instead, he may prefer to spend his disposable dough on his jujitsu classes or Amtrak tickets to visit his long-distance steady every other weekend. But if it is a severe need-want of his, I'd like to be the one to help.

You *should* have what you need-want and you shouldn't have to feel forced to pay the manufacturer's suggested retail price. So here's how to spend smarter on tech goodies. (Admittedly I dedicate a large portion of this chapter to the almighty cell phone, but the cell is a big purchase and one that comes with a *lot* of wallet-friendly options, many that we fail to embrace. I also threw in a section on how to save on a gym membership. You can thank me later.)

CELLULICIOUS

Raise your hand if you owned the Motorola Razr phone. And raise your other hand if you

1. ever wanted to throw it against the wall
2. felt you had a gun to your head while buying it
3. got ripped off
4. some or all of the above.

I'm raising both hands right now. I've even got one leg up in the air as further protest. Full disclosure: I despise the process of buying *any* cell phone involving a salesperson. Not only do they rope me into buying a piece of crap, I always have to sign my life away to a two-year-long cell plan. Two years?! Would you like my firstborn child, as well, Mr. Verizon?

But you can't *not* have a cell phone. It's practically a necessity these days. It helps us in emergency situations, like when the car breaks down, we become lost, or we need to avoid the discomfort of being alone at a bar while waiting for a friend to return from the bathroom. (*Random musing:* I once went on a date with a guy who didn't own a cell phone. He was also pretentious. I'm wondering now if that was just a coincidence.)

I understand that as you read this, you may be stuck in a two-year plan, yourself. Still, it's important to consider this advice the next time you go shopping for a new phone and plan. You could save hundreds. (That said, there are ways to get out of your contract prematurely and avoid the early termination fee, or ETF. Check out the Cut Loose . . . sidebar.)

WHAT'S FIRST? THE PHONE OR THE PLAN?

It's like the chicken/egg debate. Going cellular has two unavoidable and inevitable steps: picking a plan and then choosing a cell phone or vice versa. There's no rule that says you have to choose a phone first and a plan second, and most phones are available through all major carriers (companies like T-Mobile, AT&T, Sprint, Verizon, etc.). To help you figure out whether to start with the phone or the plan, here are some questions to consider.

Why Are You Drooling? If it's the desire for some wireless company's thousand-minutes package for $50 a month, start there and pick from its selection of phones. Or, if you've been salivating over the bells and whistles of Apple's iPhone (and presumably have the $400 odd bucks to buy the iPod/phone/video player/"babe magnet," as my old coworker Cliff at thestreet.com calls it), head straight for it, knowing that for now you will be stuck choosing AT&T as your wireless carrier.

What Are Your Friends and Family Using? The other way to begin your approach is to find out what wireless plan your friends and family members have and copy them. In some cases, signing up for the same network as friends and family can help preserve your minutes since calls made to and from them would be considered "in-network" and free. For example, if you and your mom chat three times a day for an hour at a time, those minutes may not get deducted from your overall monthly minute allowance with, say, Verizon.

Can You Make a Family? No, I'm not talking about having babies. But you may consider trying what my friend Paul, a fashion model/photographer/freelance writer in New York, did. He and his three roommates teamed up and decided to go in on a family plan with the carrier offering the best rate. From there, they bought their cell phones with the wireless company, getting two phones for free (thanks to the family plan promo) and saving hundreds of dollars on registration fees and monthly charges. Just be upfront with the salesperson.

HOW MANY MINUTES DO I BUY?

It's pretty impossible to know how many minutes *exactly* you'll eat up before you start using a phone. My advice: Imagine how many minutes you'll need based on your calling habits and the likelihood your friends will call you often during the day. Also take into account whether you mostly give out your cell, home, or office number when filling out doctor forms and bank papers, making restaurant reservations, and filling out online surveys, etc. All this might give you a sense of how many calls you'll make in a given month and just how many people out there have your cell phone number. From there, tack on at least a hundred more minutes. The best possible advice when it comes to minutes is: When in doubt, round *up*. It almost always costs less to overbuy minutes ahead of time than to go over in a given month. I repeat: Don't fall victim, because while the per-minute cost within a plan may be 5¢ to 8¢, the overage can be up to 45¢ per minute. You'll also need to guesstimate when you'll make the bulk of your calls, recognizing that plans usually include designated daytime minutes (often 7 A.M. to 7 P.M.) and anytime minutes (usually weekends and from 7 P.M. to 7 A.M.). For me, I don't need as many daytime minutes as I do nighttime because I use my work phone during the day and make the bulk of my personal calls with my cell phone at night. For example, my parents live in San Francisco—three hours behind me. I have to usually wait until 9 P.M. before reaching them at their house since they don't get home from work until 6ish. My monthly minute allotment is around nine hundred minutes. I never use it all up, but better safe than sorry.

➤ ➤ ➤ ➤ ➤ **Prepaid Possibilities**

So the section on predetermining your minute usage to guesstimate your cell plan has left you still scratching your head. Here's another suggestion: Get a prepaid phone for a few months to figure out your minute-usage tendencies before completely committing to a two-year plan. Just like a prepaid calling card, prepaid phones offer pay-as-you-go plans. AT&T, Verizon, and T-Mobile, for example, offer prepaid plans. The drawback is, of course, you don't get your pick of the fanciest phones.

➤ ➤ ➤ ➤ ➤ **Talk Ain't Cheap**

Here's some time-measuring help, based on the different voice conversations you likely have with friends, family, and your shrink on a regular basis.

CALLING DR. SHRINK

"And then in fourth grade, the other kids called me fat.": Figure 25 to 30 minutes (and $75 per hour).

"Why is my bill $750 for last month!!!?": Figure 10 minutes.

CALLING BFF

"Don't forget to bring your iPod speakers to my party.": Figure 2 to 5 minutes.

"We broke up!": Figure an hour, more if you were the one who got dumped.

CALLING MOM

"I hate my job. My boss is a big, mean jerk.": Figure 15 to 30 minutes.

"Quick! I'm at the mall. Is $300 too much for shoes?": Figure 4 seconds.

CALLING YOUR STEADY

"I miss you.": Figure 3 to 5 minutes (5 to 8 times a day).

"You're pissing me off.": Figure 15 minutes. Then hang up and set up a face-to-face.

RESPECT THY TEXT MESSAGES

I heart texting. I know people, like my tree-hugging friend Kayla, who would frown upon this. Why send a dry text when you can call and interact personally, share laughter and cry if you want to? For me, texts (1) save time, (2) avoid chatty digression that eats up precious minutes, and (3) allow me to send random sweet nothings to my steady who lives 120 miles away, without really interrupting his day. (One month I tallied more than 150 of these.) Had I known I would be such a text-crazed maniac, I would have signed up for a bigger plan. But, I had just gotten the free basic plan, which allowed for only 100 texts per month. My overage meant I had to cough up an extra 10¢ for each additional text, an additional twenty bucks that month. This happened a few months in a row until Verizon sent me a letter alerting me of my text-binging. They offered me 500 texts per month for $10 a month and I signed up immediately.

WHICH CARRIER IS THE BEST?

This is a personal question. I've used nearly all the major carrier networks and the one that suits me best currently is Verizon. I find it's got the best coverage and connectivity in New York City (plus, my parents and friends mostly use Verizon, which allows for a lot of in-network calling, which helps conserve minute usage).

When choosing a carrier, you should first and foremost make sure your bases are covered. While carriers have improved their local and national coverage over the years, dead spots still exist. Don't be caught by surprise. Make sure the carrier provides coverage not only in your home area, but also at work and places you will visit. A recent Consumer Reports survey found Verizon and T-Mobile to have the best coverage performance overall, but you should also double-check with neighbors and coworkers for your specific location(s). After you settle on a plan, you usually get a grace period of at least two weeks to test-drive the phone. Check for black holes then, too, since carriers' coverage maps are not always totally accurate.

➤ ➤ ➤ ➤ ➤ **Inside the Wireless Store:** *How to Deal*

Like when dodging annoying sales reps at the used-car lot trying to convince you to spend all your money on a '98 Accord, buying a cell plan takes a similar amount of mental preparation. (Maybe even do a few push-ups before heading inside the store.) Don't be intimidated by the sales rep, even if his name is Ike and he has eighteen tattoos (that you can see), none of which say *Mom* inside the illustration of an arrowed heart. Know you have the power to negotiate. Sometimes it helps to stretch the truth. Here are my dos and don'ts.

1. Don't go it alone. Bring a friend who'll shamelessly offer a third opinion, make intimidating faces at the sales rep, and periodically project so everyone hears, "I saw this on the Web for, like, way cheaper."

2. Do intimidate. It doesn't hurt to mention that at the same wireless store a town away, or at, say, the mall, you were offered the same plan including the same phone for free and in the limited-edition color.

3. Do quote the Web. Price shop online and print out the evidence to convince the sales rep to match the price you found on the Net. This is not an urban myth—sales reps have been known to match prices.

4. Do get the gossip. Find out what sort of deals your coworkers and friends struck to get a sense of whether you're getting screwed or not.

5. Don't bother with accessories. Sales reps need to meet quota every month and to reach their goals, they need to sell hands-free sets, leather covers, and Fat Joe ring tones. Step away. You can buy this crap later and for a lot less on the Web or at your local giant discount retailer.

6. Don't go two years if you don't wanna. You can go month-by-month. It's barely advertised, so ask. The caveat: you won't get mad discounts on cell phones, but you can buy a phone for less on the Web, like at www.ebay.com. See the next section for more shopping tips.

DO I BUY MY PHONE AND PLAN FROM THE SAME PLACE?

Don't assume you *need* to buy both directly from the same store. While the sales guy may make it seem like you don't have a choice, that you have to pick among the $400 Treo, the mediocre $150 phone, or the crap $40 phone that offers three dials—911,

Fandango, and your mom—remember, you have many, many, many more choices. Buying a phone from a carrier is usually the most expensive route, though, granted it is more convenient since you can one-stop shop. But the difference between buying a phone from the carrier to somewhere online or at a separate retail store can be as much as $200. EBay, Amazon, www.letstalk.com, and www.wirefly.com are good places to start searching for a phone online. Make sure each offer comes with a good return policy and that (duh) it is compatible with your carrier.

➤ ➤ ➤ ➤ ➤ Unlock the Magic . . . in an Hour

Your Need-Want: A new phone

Problem: Your two-year contract isn't up and switching phones with your carrier means having to cancel your contract (for a ridiculous fee) and start a new one.

Solution: Buy an "unlocked" version of the phone you want from the Web.

Huh?: An "unlocked" phone lets you take your identification from your existing cell phone and put it in the "unlocked" phone. This requires transferring your SIM, or subscriber information module, card. Not all phones use SIM cards, so this advice has its caveats.

➤ ➤ ➤ ➤ ➤ Cut Loose from Your Plan. Early. Penalty Free . . . in an Hour.

Most plans come with two-year contracts and, guess what, a lot can change in two years. You could start to hate your service, move to a new location, or need to change your number because your ex-hookup won't stop calling. But what keeps us in these horrible relationships (with the carrier, not our exes) is the gosh-awful early termination fees, which can run anywhere from $150 to $250. That's more than the cost of most standard cell phones. But I'm here to say there *are* ways to kiss off your plan and avoid breaking your piggy bank to do it.

Make an online match. You may not know this, but like with many gym memberships and even most leases, it is within your right to transfer the ownership of your cell plan to someone else. There are a growing number of third-party Web sites that play matchmaker between unhappy cell phone customers and those seeking a less-expensive, low-duration cell plan. Both www.cellswapper.com and www.celltradeUSA.com provide listings and facilitate exchanges online. It costs a fee, anywhere from around $15 to $20 to sign up, but that's a minor cost when you consider not having to pay $150 for canceling your account altogether. You can also do this yourself. Just find someone through your network of friends at work or home to see if anyone desires to pick up the remainder of your cell plan. Is there someone you know moving to your area who may need a noncommittal, quick cell phone fix? A college student in the area desperate for a short-term cell plan for a semester or two? Once you track down someone, call up your cell carrier and say you want to toss your contract over to this person. The danger of doing this switcheroo, whether independently or through a Web site, is that the carrier may not let you keep your cell phone number and apply it to another phone plan. Now, legally you *are* entitled to keep your cell phone number when you jump plans, but the law only protects you when you entirely fulfill your original plan and wait until the contract is expiring (read: not in the case of a transfer). FYI, the act of keeping your cell phone number is known as porting the number. It's a word to have handy the next time you're at the cell dealer.

Keep a close watch. Carriers have been known to offer customers a rare window of opportunity when they mess up or change the terms of your original contract. For example, when Verizon raised its text message rate, it allowed customers affected by the increase to opt out of their contract, fee free. Bottom line: The change needs to have an "adverse" effect on your current contract. In other words, if your carrier lowers fees or gives you free extra minutes, you can't use that as a bargaining chip to get out of your contract penalty free.

Get "fired." It's no guarantee, but a cell phone provider may let you loose if you become an "unprofitable" customer. For example, use your phone in a roaming area all the time or call your carrier's help operator *all the time*. (Sprint, reportedly, once fired a bunch of customers for calling its help desk too much.) Or strictly call people in your "in-network," friends and family with the same provider, to whom calls are free.

Move. Or tell your carrier that you're moving to an area with zero coverage. You'll have to prove your new address, so don't bother lying about this.

Join the army. I'm joking, but this *is* a bona fide way of getting out of your plan without a slap on the wrist. You will need to provide proof of your official orders. Also, I would stress that this decision prerequisites some serious deep thinking. Be sure it's not over a dumb phone.

Sue. If all else fails, you can sue the cell provider in small claims court for a legitimate problem, such as "lack of service" or "poor connectivity." As the very awesome Ben Popken, editor of the very helpful Consumerist .com, told me once: "Deliver the summons to one of the company's mall kiosks and win judgment by default when the company fails to show up for the court date."

GO-GO GADGET: OPT ONLINE

I can't even remember the last time I bought something at a physical electronics store (besides a cell phone store). Instead, for the real tech buys outside of cell phones, all my shopping these days happens at a few Web sites: www.ebay.com, www.amazon.com, and www.target.com. Call me weird, but I just don't have the time or the stamina to comparison shop at individual stores. I can still read dozens of reviews online, compare prices within minutes, make the purchase, and be done with it, all during a lunch break. I do believe in going into one or two stores at max and seeing the product in person, to get a better sense of size and appearance. But then I hit the Internet.

There are some cons to shopping online, though. The biggest includes the cost of shipping and handling, which, in some cases, can tack on an extra $100 to the final cost of a big-ticket item. The other risk to shopping online is buying from a nonsecure or fraudulent site. I've got a sidebar on how to avoid shady Web sites.

Here's an example of how I saved recently on the Web. I bought the Flip video camera from Amazon for my little brother, who loves posting homemade short videos with his friends on YouTube. My friend and coworker at thestreet.com, James, was showing off his Flip cam during work. This thing can record up to sixty minutes of video with pretty decent sound and visual quality, and it can all be uploaded to your computer through a simple USB cable! Love! And I knew Todd would love it, too. (I find I'm becoming more and more of a gadget fiend, as I continue working in broadcast media surrounded by genius techies.) My first step: a quick price comparison at www.shopping.com and www .bizrate.com, which discovered that www.target.com had the lowest listed price. But then I factored in shipping and found that www.amazon.com's total price would actually be less, because shipping there would be free. Done! Estimated time of purchase, including product testing, price comparing, and credit-card entering: twenty minutes tops, leaving me forty minutes to run out and grab lunch.

➤ ➤ ➤ ➤ ➤ **Is the Site Legit? Watch out!**

Before you run your credit card at a Web site, make sure it's legit and secure. Does the site's URL address begin with *https://* or does it have the official VeriSign seal of security on the home page? If you're buying from a company you're not familiar with, take a close look at its Web site. Is it well constructed, professional, and user-friendly? Can you find the information you want to know about the company and the products? Are the products clearly and completely described? Here are some red flags.

No address. Look for a street address and a telephone number, as well as e-contact information. You want off-line contact information in case you need it.

Bad services/policies. Check the company's after-sale service and support policies, as well as refund and return policies. Make sure you are willing to accept its terms if you make a purchase you're not happy with. Also check the company's privacy policy—you don't want a mailbox full of spam because you happened to buy from a company that sells its customer list.

No off-site ads. Does the online seller invest in advertising outside its Web site? This is another reassurance that the merchant is legitimate— scammers won't spend any money advertising and promoting their business. While this is tough to discover, you can start by asking friends if they've heard of the company before. You can also call the site's toll-free number and ask to speak with the sales/marketing reps.

Others have complained. Do a basic Google search on the company name and see what pops up. Just be sure to put any negative information you find in context. Even the best of companies will drop the ball once in a while and sometimes the customer's complaint isn't valid. Increasingly, companies are allowing buyers to post product reviews on their sites, and this is a great way to learn about the product and the merchant. When in doubt, you can always poke through some, if any, customer complaints at the Better Business Bureau, www.bbb.org.

➤ ➤ ➤ ➤ Protect Your ID

Identity theft is one of the fastest growing crimes in the country with some nine million incidents every year, according to the National Institute of Justice. On average, people lose more than $6,000 as a result of ID theft, according to Identity Theft 911, a consultancy that works with financial institutions to prevent identity theft. That's double the average amount stolen in an armed robbery. Although most cases of identity theft actually occur off-line, ID theft often comes up in conversations about online purchasing. You need to cover all your bases when it comes to protection. Here's a prevention plan.

Play it safe online. Experts say to avoid storing personal data on laptops. They also recommend shopping online only at trusted and secure Web vendors. The URL or Web address should begin with *https* instead of simply *http://*. Additionally, look for a secure "sign." Different Web browsers have different symbols either at the top or bottom corners of their Web-pages. For example, Firefox shows a padlock icon in the bottom right corner of the browser. Safari displays a padlock in the top right corner of the browser. Explorer will show a small padlock in the bottom center.

Secure your ID off-line. Most ID theft happens off the Internet, with thieves getting your personal information the old-fashioned way: from your wallet or purse or by rummaging through your trash. Experts suggest cutting out the address labels on your magazines and shredding any material that's got your personal information on it, such as credit-card solicitations. And never carry around pay stubs, deposit slips, and receipts.

Guard your SSN. Almost never enter this information on a Web site, unless perhaps when you're filing your taxes online. Beyond that, don't carry your Social Security card in your wallet or purse. And never, ever write the number on checks.

Get your boss to help. Employers should do their part as well. Make sure your company doesn't use your Social Security number as an employee ID number.

Check your credit. Monitor all your credit-card purchases and have your credit-card company alert you if and when any suspicious activity occurs. Also keep a close eye on your credit report on a regular basis for any unusual changes. And be sure to obtain a free credit report. Remember from chapter 3, "Banking in Bed and Scoring," you're entitled to one from each of the three credit-reporting agencies annually. Visit www.annualcreditreport.com.

Report immediately. Prevention is your best weapon, but it's not completely fail-safe. If you find yourself a victim of identity theft, reporting it immediately will help minimize your losses. Contact the Federal Trade Commission at 1-877-ID THEFT (438–4338) or fill out a complaint form at the FTC's Web site, www.ftc.gov. And in case you've lost your Social Security card, contact the Social Security Administration at www.ssa.gov for a replacement.

EBAY MADE EASY

My proudest purchase on eBay was the 1999 "The End" Beanie Baby for my then eight-year-old brother. To this day, he says it was his happiest gift-opening moment ever. That winter, the stores were all sold out of this top Christmas item, and my parents, being the late-adopters to the World Wide Web that they were, were up in arms about how to attain the limited-edition stuffed animal that my little brother had been asking for from every white-bearded, red-suited man in the malls. I, meanwhile, bought it for $35 on eBay when my parents had said they'd seen it in random stores (before it was completely sold out) selling for more than $100. In short, eBay is awesome. My favorite thing to buy on the world's biggest online auction site is underwear. No joke. A few vendors on the site sell Hanky Panky underwear for a 40 percent discount. (If you don't know what I'm talking about, ladies, Google it. Then buy a pair for yourself. Your life will change for the better.) Um, where were we? . . . Oh yes, eBay is great for finding the hard-to-find for much less than many sites. It's a proven fact. But even though eBay is amazing, there are tricks and tips to help you be a better buyer on the site. Consider these:

Snipe It. Savvy auction bidders wait until the last few seconds of the auction and use "sniping" tools (www.powersnipe.com and www.ezsniper.com offer downloadable services) that do the bidding for them just before the auction ends. This can minimize competition and keep prices slightly lower. You can also monitor the auction real time to place last-minute bids if necessary.

Then there's eBay's proxy bidding system. You simply enter the maximum amount you're willing to pay, and eBay will automatically increase your bid by the standard increments until it hits that amount. So, let's say the most you want to pay for a used

MacBook Pro is $700. Your proxy bid would then be $700. If no one outbids you, you win the MacBook Pro for the last bid offer, which may be substantially less than $700. Otherwise, you'll be notified if/when someone beats your proxy bid. At that time you can place a higher bid or you can pass.

Buy It Now. There are several versions of eBay's Buy It Now (BIN) feature. Some Buy It Now items are only sold at fixed prices and not auctioned. When you find one of those you like, if the price is right, buy it before someone else does.

Auctions can also have BIN options, but this opportunity to buy immediately disappears the instant someone places a bid. So if you spot a great Buy It Now price in an auction, purchase the item immediately.

First Browse the "New." Some sellers don't know the value of what they are selling. A great trick is to browse selling categories sorted by "newly listed" looking for underpriced BIN items and pouncing when you find a bargain. Just be certain you understand the condition of the item, shipping costs, and other considerations that could explain the low BIN price before you commit to purchasing.

Don't Get Too Emotional. Don't get carried away. Unless it is a very rare item (say an original iPod[!] or a seventies-era camera), another will come along next week or next month. Never bid more than you think something is worth just because you want one. There will almost certainly be others (maybe even better ones) offered on eBay in the next few weeks or months. Oh, and never bid on eBay items after your second glass of wine!

A key point here is that as a shopper, you should decide how much you're willing to pay for something and then stop bidding if the price goes over that amount. There are very few one-of-a-kind items out there; if the price gets too high, let that one go and search for another one.

THE STUDENT ID THAT KEEPS ON GIVING

If you're not sure where you left your student ID since graduating from college, I seriously recommend you track it down, especially if its expiration date is still valid. I started Penn State in 1998 and my ID said it expired in 2007. Granted, we had a lot of super-seniors on campus and five-plus years was more than typical, but I'd like to think that someone in the student ID office was looking out for me, knowing that one day I would want to buy the latest Apple device or some other tech gadget, and my ID would come to the financial rescue. Indeed, three years after graduating, it did. Don't tell Steve Jobs, but I was able to use my old college ID to get the "student" discount at Apple. The savings came to $100 off an iBook plus a credit of $250 toward the purchase of an iPod. I chose the mini iPod because it was exactly $250 and therefore *free* with the use of my credit.

No, I don't feel guilty for pretending I was a "student." In theory, I am a student of the world, right? And technically, all that the store required to see was my college ID, which hadn't yet expired. I even suspected the sales guy was onto me, since I looked nothing like my ID photo taken back in 1998. But he ran the discount through anyway, no questions asked. And I actually did this *twice*.

Two years later I went back into the Apple store. (After I accidentally dropped my first iBook on the floor and cracked the screen. Oops.) I tried to use my warranty, but Apple's warranty apparently does not cover the sort of physical damage my computer went through (whatever). It was going to cost me $800 to replace the screen, at which point I figured I'd spend an extra few hundred and buy a brand-new MacBook. Lo and behold, the "student" promotion still existed, and because my Penn State ID was still valid, I was, again, able to knock $100 off my laptop purchase and go home with a free, sleeker, *Nano* iPod this time. Come to think of it now, I've never ever paid for an iPod.

Beyond Apple, back-to-school "student" promos are popular at many stores, like Best Buy, Circuit City, and Fry's between August and October. And with a proper student ID you may be able to save a bundle. For more of an effect, strap on your old L.L. Bean backpack and don't wash your hair for a week. You'll definitely pass the test.

➤ ➤ ➤ ➤ ➤ Almost New = Often a Deal

Refurbished. The first time I researched refurbished goods, I was twenty-three and working at *Money Magazine*. Not exactly the most exciting material to be investigating, just the word alone sounds dull: *refurbished*; sounds like *defibrillator*, I remember thinking. Anyways . . . my conclusion? Don't pooh-pooh refurbished goods. It basically means the item was used once and returned to the manufacturer, mostly because consumers are indecisive and have a habit of impulse buying, only later to realize they don't really need a limited-edition Krups espresso maker. In other cases, the item just needed some patchwork or a cleanup or both. Fortunately for all other consumers interested in a Krups (or enter your must-have electric appliance/product here), stores can't legally put returned items back on the shelves as "new." Instead, they must be labeled as "previously owned" or "refurbished" and as a result are often tagged 10 to 30 percent less than brand-new products.

The advantage of buying refurbished versus "used" is that most refurbished items come with a manufacturer's warranty of at least thirty days. If the item is sans-warranty, forget it. It's not worth the 10 percent discount if there's no way to recover if/when the appliance fails you. The refurbished market includes everything from Dell PCs to Callaway golf clubs, from plasma TVs to kitchen appliances. Think twice before buying a refurbished cell phone, though. If you see one labeled as such, bet the cell phone manufacturer didn't in fact "refurbish" it, since most cell companies donate used phones to charity. It's not worth the extra cost to them, I'm told.

Open/restocked. Many electronics that have been returned to a store are put back up for sale at a discounted price, even if the item hasn't been used at all. The discount comes because the product has been opened and the box is resealed. All the parts and components should still be intact. Again, make sure any returns you buy are covered by a warranty.

Display models. Floor models (the ones put on display or used as "tester" items) are usually offered at deeply discounted prices. When buying floor models, make sure all of the accessories are included (i.e., manuals, batteries, etc.) and make sure the item has warranty coverage.

Note: If there is no warranty automatically included, you can usually ask the salesperson to throw it in because you're taking a slightly used model.

And there's always "like new" items for sale on www.amazon.com (e.g., books and DVDs) at considerably less than the list price.

PHYSCALLY FIT: HOW TO WIN AT THE GYM

I know that approximately a half hour on the treadmill at a 6.5-mile-per-hour pace burns approximately 330 calories. That's approximately one cinnamon raisin–swirl bagel from Starbucks on the way to work. I get *that* math. But what confused me for the longest time, to the point where I just felt defeated by my own indecisiveness, was whether it was worth keeping my gym membership. Was I better off using New York's Central Park for free as my workout grounds? But what about the wintertime? It gets dark early and I can't breathe properly while running in the cold. (Note: I will find any excuse not to work out. I'd rather clean toilet bowls.)

I started a gym plan in 2003 after graduating from graduate school. It cost me about $80 a month using my Time Inc. corporate ID badge (a savings of about $30 a month). But after a few years of an on-again, off-again relationship with the New York Sports Club (my attendance being more off than on), I ended my plan. For one thing, I was bitter about the $80. As an undergrad, I had spent just twenty bucks a semester at Penn State and had access to all the campus gym facilities, including tennis courts, swimming pools, and yoga classes. It was just too good to pass up. I had no excuse, actually, but to sign up. Plus, back then I had something called *time*, which allowed me the freedom to spend an hour or two at the gym (not every day, but at least three or four) and really burn some calories. I had only fifteen credits my last semester in college and, coincidentally, killer abs.

But now that I'm in New York, my choices for a plan range from $90 to as much as $250 a month, depending on which snooty gym I want to join. (If money was no concern, I'd join the Reebok Sports Club across from where Regis and Kelly tape their show. It's where all the celebs go.) I'm also time strapped and too tired to go to the gym after work. I also have to wake up superearly, so going *before* work is not an option since the gym isn't open at 4:30 A.M. At the end of the day, I would much rather run outside, when I feel like it. I also realized (after three years, no less) that, really, I only use the treadmill and a soft mat for sit-ups when I go to the gym. I don't care for the classes or the fancy towels. Thus, attending a private gym, for me, was a waste of money, considering $90 a month is also the same as $1,080 a year, which is also one awesome four-day weekend in Aspen or a substantial stake in Jamba Juice (JMBA), which at the time of writing this book trades at around $9 per share.

All said, the downside of no gym membership is that during the winter I risk the danger of sitting on my butt indoors where it's warm. I don't run much during Dec.–Feb. because of the frost and usually end up putting on an extra two or three pounds. Okay five. But you also have to factor in all that holiday turkey and pie and those candy canes.

Here are some ways to save on a gym passport, should you choose to go. (Another incentive to joining the gym: My friend Rennie met her fiancé at one. It's not the *worst* place to meet people, I suppose. Think of all the money some spend on Saturday nights barhopping trying to score dates.)

Taste Test

Just like with cell plans, comparison shop for the best convenience and services/amenities at a few gyms before committing to any one club's plan. Most offer prospective clients free day passes or even a week's worth of access to their facilities and classes. While trying out a gym, take into account what time you're likely to go and how long it may take you to drive/walk there from your office or home. And while you're shopping around, let the gym's membership consultant know you're shopping around. The smell of competition might win you some good deals.

Don't You Know Who I Am?

Many gyms offer discounts for students, senior citizens (I know, that's not you . . . but someday?), corporate employees, or anyone who lives or works in the same building as the gym. Where I work, at thestreet.com, I qualify for special discount at the Equinox next door. It still adds up to $140 a month, but the savings there, and in many similar cases, can be as much as 40 percent. Additionally, if you are someone who will use the gym during off-peak hours (i.e., after the morning rush and not after work), some gyms may offer you discounted memberships.

Join When It's Hot, Hot, Hot

Ignore all that January "New Year, New You" marketing which hopes to fool you into signing up for a "limited"-time deal. The summer months are the slowest times for gyms and, therefore, the best time to strike deals. The gym owners already know they'll get people in January because that's inevitably when most weight resolutions are made. They don't need to lower their prices at that point. What's more: Wait until the *last* day of the month to join, since salespeople typically have monthly quotas to fill and may offer better deals to get you to sign.

Read Finely the Fine Print

The contract isn't often that long-winded, but be aware of some of the policy requirements the buff sales agent may "forget" to mention or that you fail to hear while she's wooing you with a tour of the gym's heated pool and power Pilates session. For example, some gyms require automatic payment through a bank account or credit card. Watch out for any related finance charges that the gym may tack on. Also, be familiar with the gym's cancellation policy. Some don't let you cancel until your contract expires—if you want out, you have to find someone to take your membership, which, of course, has a cost. Others may slap on a hefty fee, like a cell plan does, if you cancel your contract before a set date. My mom was paying just $10 a month for her gym membership back when my parents were living in Massachusetts. Awesome, right?

Little did she know the el cheapo plan obligated her to stay on for two years. What was this, Sprint? When she and my dad moved out West a year into her contract, the gym operator wanted proof of her new address (which wasn't that hard to produce). But they also wanted a copy of the deed to her new house and her Iranian birth certificate. It was like an episode of Monty Hall's *Let's Make a Deal.*

Consider à la Carte

A U.C. Berkeley/Stanford University study found that average gym members visited their fitness clubs just four times a month. That's once a week. Considering monthly memberships can cost as much as $150 a month, you may want to nix the full-time membership and pay as you go. Gyms typically charge nonmembers $20 to $25 for a one-day pass.

LUCKY MONEY

A way to make money effortlessly and unexpectedly.

Find money. Keep money.

ADULTS ONLY!

Undressing the Financial Market

Warning: This chapter contains mature content not suitable for those who take pleasure in continuing to sleep in their twin bed at Mommy and Daddy's. Rather, it is intended for young adults who believe the finest route to financial security is investing—and beginning to invest while you're *young*. It's not enough to stash your money in a savings account, even if it's yielding a competitive 5 percent annually, and it's not enough to have just a 401(k) or an IRA. Stocks, bonds, mutual funds, and other investment instruments should not be excluded from your money management portfolio, especially if you're planning on boosting your current disposable income and retiring strong. The compound interest earned in a savings account can be impressive, but nothing beats the potential gains in the stock market. Let's face it: If we want to live comfortably in retirement, we have to be aggressive with growing our money today. After all, we're expected to live longer, Social Security is more or less going down the drain, pensions are a thing of the past, and healthcare costs are soaring. Not to mention, a modest condo in La Jolla, California (where I dream of retiring), costs in the neighborhood of $1 million. Hey, a girl can dream, can't she?

Even if you're surviving paycheck to paycheck and can't fathom how you could trade stocks, keep reading anyway. Who knows, you may see that it *is* possible to invest now, or at the very least you'll pick up a thing or two about how financial investments *work*, which can score some brownie points with your boss, who's probably just starting to grapple stocks (slowpoke). Consider this chapter as essential background and advice for when you decide to tackle the investment world, be it today or down the road.

Full disclosure: I'm no certified stock-picking expert and I don't trade individual stocks. My career as a financial reporter makes it unethical to trade stocks (besides shares of thestreet.com, where I work), since I'm privy to more juicy information than the average Joe. But with a degree in finance and years reporting on the stock market, I'm confidently in the know about the basics (and then some). It's partly through osmosis, partly because I pay close attention to one particular investing guru, Jim Cramer, the cofounder of www.thestreet.com and my frequent guest on *Wall Street Confidential* on thestreet.com TV. Jim also hosts *Mad Money* on CNBC, where each weeknight he educates viewers on how to make money in the market, whether the stock market is going up, down, or sideways. His animated antics on TV (e.g., flying chicken props, crying-baby sound effects) have a whole nation captivated—primarily twenty-something-year-olds, believe it or not. My brother, a junior in high school, and his friends also go *booyah* for the Cramer. What does that tell me? Investing advice should not be reserved for rich folks or baby boomers looking for a crash course to greater retirement wealth. More youngins are hungry to invest, so please give us what we want.

To that point, I feel fortunate to bring you the genius advice of Jim Cramer at the end of this chapter (saving the best for last). He's someone who understands the stock market like a scientist and a psychologist, a teacher and a student. Plus, Jim makes it fun.

Ahead of that, here are some stock market basics to get you warmed up, provided by yours truly.

STOCKS 101

Getting Acquainted. As Jim Cramer emphasizes later on in this chapter, it's important to *want* to be in the stock market. Just as we spend time hunting down an apartment, searching for a job, shopping for a car, or planning a dream vacation, we need to be dedicated to learning about the business world and the stocks we are interested in holding. The Web sites www.thestreet.com (of course), finance.yahoo.com, www.nytimes.com, www.nypost .com, and online.wsj.com are my go-to sites every morning to get the latest business news. If there's something that catches my interest and I want more analysis, I do a blog search on that topic and always, always visit www.stockpickr.com (a site created by my friend James Altucher and owned by thestreet.com). Stockpickr is the Facebook for stock lovers. It's a social-networking utility that connects investors and wannabe investors. You can literally look up the portfolios of investing titans such as Warren Buffett and George Soros as well as everyday stock pickers. Here you can also send your questions to the Stockpickr community, including Jim Cramer and James Altucher, who among other activities runs a fund of funds. James has always told me he first learned how to invest by mimicking the moves of investment pros including Buffett (his book *Trade Like Warren Buffett* tells all). James invented Stockpickr to bring that same idea of portfolio transparency to the masses. Time.com voted it one of the fifty best new Web sites of 2006. It's definitely worth your time to check it out.

WHAT TO BUY?

Some Value, Lots of Growth (a Few Specs). Traditional investment portfolios have a range of securities, from stocks and bonds to mutual funds and exchange-traded funds (we'll get to these a little later on). Your portfolio should be adjusted for diversity several times over the years, as your risk tolerance shifts. And since risk has an adverse relationship to age (the younger you are, the more risk you should take on), now is the time to gamble (a little) with stocks.

The older you are, the more advice you'll hear about investing in *value* versus *growth* stocks and mutual funds. Value stocks have outperformed growth stocks in the long term and are, therefore, considered "less risky." In fact, from 1969 to 2006, value stocks outpaced growth stocks by an average of 2.5 percent each year, according to Ibbotson Associates. Value stocks typically have a high dividend yield and less volatility or fluctuation in price. They include many of the so-called blue chip stocks, or household companies listed on the Dow Jones Industrial Average, such as Altria, Procter & Gamble, and General Electric.

But you can afford more risk when you're young. Growth stocks and mutual funds usually comprise relatively younger companies whose earnings are growing fast—think tech stocks like Cisco, Baidu, and Apple. These stocks can be pretty volatile, or have major price swings, since they require more guesswork by investors. Any bit of news can seriously affect price levels. Why? It's harder to value growth stocks because there's not a lot of historical performance data. Investors go more on how they think or perceive the stock will perform based on demand or projected demand for the company's product or service. "Growth stocks trade more on investor psychology," as James Altucher tells me.

Your start-up portfolio should have a combination of value and growth stocks, but in your twenties you want to focus more on growth stocks because these may build your wealth faster in the short term. And you'll have more time to recover losses if your picks fail you. Once you're more settled in life (i.e., married with dependents), the general advice shifts to having a more value-oriented portfolio with a selection of bonds as well. The closer you get to retirement, the less chancy you want to be with your money.

But back to being young and fabulous: For where we are in life, we should be more aggressive and invest mainly in growth stocks and funds, and don't forget, *speculative* stocks. Speculative stocks are the riskiest kind. They're typically small cap (short for small capitalization), meaning the shares outstanding total less than $1 billion. These companies are not in the big leagues, yet. They're more volatile, which means they are more likely to have severe price fluctuations. Also, they have relatively less professional analyst coverage. That said, these stocks often hinge on certain probabilities and if they turn out in the companies' favor, the stocks could explode. For example, some biotechnology companies are highly speculative. Their stocks sometimes trade around $3 to $10 per share, but can soar on, say, FDA approval of a drug. Micro-cap stocks, with less than $250 million market capitalization, are considered to be among the riskiest stocks. My friend Tim Sykes turned $12,000 of his Bar Mitzvah money into $1.65 million by the time he was a freshman in college. How he did it? Many, many micro-cap bets.

Now, because your entire life shouldn't be a gamble (think: cost of La Jolla, three-bedroom condo, year 2045), you need some investments that can be more of a sure thing, more secure financial instruments, like medium- to large-cap stocks, which include Microsoft, eBay, McDonald's, and Wal-Mart. I am not recommending these stocks, just giving you a sense of the size of the companies that fit in these categories. Your portfolio should also be dedicated to bonds, mutual funds, and exchange-traded funds, which are less risky and offer more long-term gains. You don't have to go too crazy with these, but it's good to start getting acquainted and building your portfolio now little by little.

HOW TO BUY?

Through the Internet, of course! We do everything else online, so buying investments should be no exception. Like a smart consumer, you want to shop around and consider your options before settling with an online brokerage site. All these sites, from TD Ameritrade to E*Trade, have different sign-up costs, trading fees, and investment opportunities. Weigh each offer carefully and scour the Web sites during trading hours (9:30 A.M. to 4:00 P.M.) to see how fast they load and whether the links make fast connections. A caveat to online trading is that your trades are not executed immediately after you click the mouse or hit Enter. It can take anywhere from forty-five seconds to twenty minutes to fully execute a market order due to a jam of other orders ahead of yours. So, while you think you're buying a hundred shares of eBay stock at $31.92 per share because that was the best available price when you sent in your request, the slowdown may cause the transaction to occur at the *next* obtainable price, say $32.22. That's 30¢ more! To help you better evaluate online brokerages, I've made a little crib sheet of the most popular ones.

Scottrade. The number one–ranked site by J.D. Power and Associates for six years running based on cost, trade execution, Web site capability, and customer service, among other criteria. The site requires a $500 initial investment to start an account and charges $7 per stock trade. It's good for those who want some hand-holding.

Each account comes with a free membership to a local branch office equipped with a personal broker available to answer questions.

TD Ameritrade. To start an account, you need to invest at least $2,000 (except for an IRA account, which costs a minimum of $1,000). The site charges a $15 quarterly account maintenance fee if your account has less than $2,000 in liquid assets. Each Internet stock trade costs $9.99.

E*TRADE. Investors need at least $1,000 to open an account. The site is better for active traders; there's a $40 fee if the account holder makes zero trades in the quarter or if the account has less than $10,000 in assets. Stock trades cost $6.99 to $12.99 each, depending on the size of the account and the frequency of trades per quarter.

Zecco. A relatively newbie to the online trading arena, Zecco is growing rapidly. Since October 2006, there have been 85,000 individual accounts opened on the site. The name is short for Zero Cost Commission, which is true. Zecco doesn't charge you a commission for stocks and exchange-traded funds, or ETFs (promise, more on this later). You also get ten free trades per month. The caveat: Your account balance needs to be at least $2,500. If your account is less than $2,500, it costs $4.50 per trade. No-load mutual fund trades cost $10.

Get Your Feet Wet ➤

The site www.investingonline.org offers an Investing Simulator Center that lets consumers get their feet wet with some virtual trades.

➤ ➤ ➤ ➤ ➤ **Avoid Unintentional Trades**

Talk about wasted money. Like the time you booked your flight from L.A. to Boston for Saturday the twelfth instead of Saturday the nineteenth. Check your order twice before sending it through because once it's done, it's done, and just like the country's embattled airlines, the financial market is not sympathetic if you want your money back. Know these common terms before placing an order on a Web-based brokerage.

- ➤ A *limit order* is an order to buy or sell a number of shares of a stock at a specific price or at a better price. For example, you place a limit order on www.zecco.com to buy ten shares of Apple at $82 or less or to sell ten shares of Apple at $90 or more.
- ➤ A *market order* seeks the best price available at the time the order is executed in the trading marketplace. Be prepared that this price may not be the last price you saw and wanted on finance.yahoo .com. Why? Because stock prices can experience huge shifts in a single moment and can be as volatile as, I dunno, your bipolar beauty pageant roommate sophomore year at Penn State. I'm just saying.
- ➤ A *stop order* is an order to buy or sell a stock once it hits a certain price, called the stop price. At that point, the stop order becomes a market order and is subject to shifts in the market, as described above.
- ➤ A *stop-limit order* combines a stop and a limit order, as the name implies. Here, you can protect yourself from the risk of not getting in at a specific price. Once the stock hits the stop price, the stop-limit order turns into a plain limit order, which lets you buy or sell shares at a specific or better price.

THE ANATOMY OF A STOCK

You adore Whole Foods. You love its aisles of organic frozen dinners and Kashi cereal. You love that the company is so eco-friendly, that its employees seem so happy, and that you can get cash back at the register. Maybe this is a stock worth buying? Well, you're somewhat on the right path. But never assume that just because you like a company, its stock will love you back. Many experts—including Jim Cramer—tell me it's dangerous to get emotional when investing in stocks. You need to detach yourself from the attractiveness of a company's product or service and examine its financial health. Still, I think there is *some* correlation between one's *impression* of a company and the health of its stock. In the end, it's important to buy what you know, not just on the outside, but also on the inside. You want to buy a stock that won't tank as soon as you buy it, too. (Duh.) So how do you evaluate stocks? Below I give the anatomy of a stock. The goal here is that the next time you look up a stock's symbol, or ticker, on www.thestreet.com, you'll be able to make a quick assessment of its company, its overall performance, and whether the stock is worth a closer look. It's by no means the end-all of all ways to value a stock, but it's a fine start.

P/B, or Price-to-Book Ratio. This compares the company's most recent stock price versus its most recent quarterly book value per share. The book value is basically what would be given to shareholders if the company was liquidated, or acquired, and had its liabilities settled and assets sold. In other words, it's the total assets minus liabilities. The P/B, therefore, is equal to the stock price divided by the book value. In general, stocks that trade with a P/B of less than 1 are considered undervalued . . . which may mean there's something wrong with the books, or it may mean it's a bargain!

Market Capitalization. This tells you how many shares outstanding the company has on the open market. It's a good gauge of a company's *size*, relative to its competitors.

Dividend. A kickback. Value companies sometimes give shareholders a little somethin' when the stock performs well. This can be paid in either more stock or cash. It's considered taxable income.

Earnings Per Share, aka EPS. This tells you how profitable or unprofitable a company currently is. It's equal to the company's latest profit (or earnings minus dividends on preferred stock) divided by the average number of shares outstanding, or the number of shares currently up for grabs by investors in the market. Publicly traded companies must report quarterly earnings that include their most recent earnings per share. Each year, they'll also issue the full year's earning per share.

P/E, or Price-to-Earnings Ratio. Ever hear a stock be called too expensive or so cheap? That's typically a reference to the price-to-earnings ratio, aka the P/E ratio or earnings multiple. It's how much, at the end of the day, the market will pay for the stock. This number is equal to the stock's current price divided by its earnings per share, or EPS, from the past twelve months. For example, if Whole Foods (ticker: WFMI) is trading around $50 per share and its earnings per share is $1.50, then its P/E is around 33. It's one way to compare a company to others in a similar industry, or to the Standard & Poor's 500, the broader market benchmark, but it shouldn't be the only factor taken into consideration. That's a big mistake.

THE WORLD BEYOND STOCKS

Yes, there's a whole galaxy. Hold on tight.

Mutual Funds

More college students are getting in on the mutual fund band-wagon. The two biggest pluses are that they offer diversification like almost no other asset class and the minimum investment for some mutual funds start around $1,000 or less, which gives us an ability to participate.

When you buy a mutual fund, you're essentially becoming a shareholder in that fund. The fund is managed by one person or a team of people, and that's not free. The Securities and Exchange Commission has a mutual fund cost calculator online at www.sec .gov/investor/tools/mfcc/mfcc-int.htm.

One big *oops* investors make is forgetting to get the prospectus of the mutual fund they're thinking of buying. Why is it important? The prospectus has some pretty important information about the fund's investment goals, its objectives, how it diversifies, the risks, the fees, and who manages and advises the fund.

Starter Mutual Funds

Here are some funds, and their ticker symbols, that focus primarily on stocks and that let you start with $1,000.

AIM Basic Value (GTVLX)

AIM European Small Company (ESMAX)

Oakmark Fund (OAKMX)

Permanent Portfolio (PRPFX)

Van Kampen Equity and Income (ACEIX)

Bonds

Or, as I like to call them, the financial stepchildren. Bonds are not as sexy as stocks. In fact, they're kind of nerdy. Like, remember that $100 savings bond you got at your Bar Mitzvah from your no-longer favorite aunt? The bond you couldn't touch until you were eighteen and then when you finally reached the voting age, you learned it had appreciated a whopping 6 percent? Awesome. That probably wasn't enough to cover your first week in college.

On the plus side, as a long-term investment, bonds carry less risk than stocks. In fact, on average, bonds attract the risk-averse—investors who can't afford to gamble. Because of their relative security and safety as compared with stocks, bonds are often used as savings vehicles for down payments on a home, college education, or retirement.

So, what are they exactly? They're IOUs: debt instruments issued by corporations and the government to raise money via the public. After all, you and I aren't the only ones who need to borrow money. Bonds are usually sold in increments of $1,000.

The safest are generally government bonds, called treasuries because they're issued by the Treasury Department. They include treasury notes, bills, and bonds, which vary based on their maturities. Some experts call government bonds the safest in the world. After all, the government will always come up with the money to pay you. That's why we pay taxes, right?

When we buy bonds, we're essentially lending our money to the issuer with the promise of getting paid the "face value" of the bond when it expires, or matures. On top of that, we can assume getting paid fixed interest during the life of the bond, which can range anywhere from three months to thirty years.

When you purchase a bond, all the conditions are laid out, including how much was lent, the interest, and the term of the bond. These things are engraved in stone. A bond is essentially a pact with the issuer that it has to pay you or it goes bankrupt.

As with stocks, you can buy bonds through brokers. Prices on more than twenty thousand bonds are listed at www.finra.org/Regulatory/Systems/TRACE/index.htm. The government also has a Web site, www.treasurydirect.gov, that sells bonds online.

You can sell bonds, too, before they expire. But because bond prices fall when interest rates rise, selling before maturity may come at a loss.

While government bonds are pretty secure, corporate bonds are more risky because investors can lose their principal if a corporation

---

Urban Dictionary for Bonds

CALL PROVISION: The stipulation that the issuer can call back the bond before it matures and pay you back with interest to date. This usually happens when interest rates fall and the company wants to issue new bonds with lower coupon rates.

COUPON RATE: The regular interest promised by the issuer.

FACE/PAR VALUE: The face value of a bond or stock. If you're lucky and/or smart, you'll be able to purchase *below par*. Like the time I convinced my neighbor Ashley to trade me her Strawberry Shortcake doll for a beat-up Barbie. The Strawberry Shortcake went for $55 on eBay twelve years later.

MATURITY: Date when a bond expires.

PUT PROVISION: Stipulation that the bondholder has the right to "put" the bond back to the issuer before maturity. This usually occurs when interest rates have gone up and the bondholder wants to take on newer bonds that offer higher rates.

defaults on a bond. The upside to corporate bonds is they usually pay more interest. Credit-rating agencies like Moody's and Standard and Poor's rate bonds on a scale of AAA (the best) to "junk" status. Junk bonds are issued by struggling companies, and they carry high risks but potentially high returns.

Index Funds

If you're low-maintenance and passive-aggressive, don't want to actively manage your portfolio or pay an expert to try to outpace the market, but still want to make a decent return on your investment, consider index funds. These are low-risk mutual funds that track a particular market index, like the Standard & Poor's 500.

The main advantage is cost, since index funds are not aggressively managed by pros. They carry expense ratios of less than 0.5 percent (i.e., the percentage of total fund assets used to cover any expenses related to running the fund). That's much lower than the 1.3–2.5 percent often charged by fund managers. The caveat: If the market tumbles, so may your index fund. The advice: Buy and hold.

Vanguard and Fidelity are two popular brands. Here's a rundown of a few of their most recommended and widely held index funds:

THE VANGUARD 500 INDEX
Ticker: VFINX
Minimum Initial Investment: $3,000
Expense Ratio: 0.18 percent

This fund is designed to track the performance of the Standard & Poor's 500 Index, which consists of five hundred of the country's biggest companies, including Google, Apple, and Staples. As of this writing, the Vanguard 500 had a year-to-date return of about 4.43 percent; the actual S&P 500 has returned roughly 4 percent.

VANGUARD TOTAL STOCK MARKET INDEX FUND (VANGUARD.COM)
Ticker: VTSMX
Minimum Initial Investment: $3,000
Expense Ratio: 0.19 percent

This fund tracks the U.S. Broad Market Index, which is made up of nearly all common stocks in the United States. It's best for long-term investors who want exposure to the broad market. The fund had returned 5.43 percent year-to-date.

FIDELITY SPARTAN 500 INDEX (FIDELITY.COM)
Ticker: FSMKX
Minimum Initial Investment: $10,000
Expense Ratio: 0.10 percent

A classic, according to most financial planners. Like the Vanguard Index 500, this index follows the S&P 500. Year-to-date, the Fidelity Spartan 500 had returned 4.2 percent. Top holdings in the fund include General Electric, Exxon Mobil, and Citigroup.

➤ ➤ ➤ ➤ **An Index for the Social Good**

Socially responsible investments, or SRIs, often comprise various companies that are passionate about social and environmental issues and attentive to their shareholders. The companies usually invest some of their money into their local communities, too.

The Domini Index, for example, is an SRI with roughly $1.8 billion in assets. The portfolio manager there invests in companies that file shareholder resolutions, are engaged in long-term dialogue, are against sweatshops and global warming, and promote diversity. In 2006, the Domini Index returned close to 3 percent.

Exchange-Traded Funds, or ETFs

Once, when I was interviewing a well-educated woman for thestreet.com, I learned that she thought an ETF was some type of UFO. Seriously, I have it on tape. So don't feel badly if you don't know what these are. Exchange-traded funds, or ETFs, are the latest investing craze, and like an index fund, an ETF tracks a benchmark. But it offers more flexibility than traditional index or mutual funds because, like stocks, it can be bought and sold throughout the day.

The downside with ETFs: As with stocks, you have to pay a commission to buy and sell an ETF. Hot examples of ETFs: the Vanguard 500 Index (ticker: VFINX) and the SPDR S&P 500 (ticker: SPY). Both track the S&P 500 Index and require a $10,000 initial investment.

Employee Stock Options

Stock options are no longer exclusively reserved for top-tier execs. More employers are granting them to rank-and-file workers, as part of an overall compensation plan you may receive upon being hired. Basically, a stock option gives you the right, or "option," to buy a certain number of shares of your employer's stock at a "strike price," which is predetermined and typically offered at a discount.

The option usually has a fixed term of between five and ten years. There's usually also a "vesting" term attached to the stock option, which controls how much an employee can exercise the option per year.

Let's say your boss gives you a hundred shares of your company's stock with a strike price of $10 per share to be used by

January 2015 on a 25 percent per year vesting schedule. This means you have the option to purchase up to twenty-five shares of your company's stock each January 1 at $10 per share, for one hundred total shares, by January 2015. After that, the option expires and can no longer be exercised.

Relative to investing in the regular stock market, exercising stock options can carry less risk. The most significant benefit is that you can decide to invest in your company's stock after knowing how the stock performed. There's no huge downside. If the stock price goes down, you can just let the option expire with no cost to you.

Not to Be Confused with . . .

There's often some confusion between employee stock options and employee stock purchase plans (ESPPs). As an eligible employee, you can elect to use the ESPP to effectively issue yourself stock options, as opposed to a regular stock option plan, in which your employer decides whether you receive option awards and how much.

With an ESPP, workers can purchase stock in their company through payroll deduction over a particular offering period, often six months.

Typically, employees can allocate 1 to 10 percent of their pay toward an ESPP. The amount is not tax deductible, but the advantage is you don't have to deal with the alternative minimum tax (AMT) when you buy and sell stock under an ESPP.

What the heck is the *AMT*? It's awfully complicated, but basically speaking, it's an additional tax some people have to pay on top of their regular income tax. The original notion behind the AMT was to prevent the rich from using tax benefits to avoid paying their taxes. But if you've heard of the AMT recently, like on the five o'clock news, it's because everyday mom-and-pop folks, who aren't rich, are trapped paying the AMT.

On the plus side, if the stock rallies in the market to $15 per share and you have the option to buy it for $10 per share, you can essentially buy the stock, then sell it for market value and make a $5-per-share gain.

➤ ➤ ➤ ➤ ➤ **Passion Plays**

So I know I said never to mix business with pleasure when it comes to stocks. Don't get emotional! But this section on "alternative investments" makes for cool bar talk or something to impress your boss with the next time you're stuck in an elevator with her. For many investors (typically wealthy ones), the following alternative strategies have made impressive returns. When you're an ace investor and have some extra cash to toy with, consider these passion plays.

Wine lovers. Fine-wine investment funds generally include wines from different countries and, sometimes, wine-distribution companies. It's most popular in Europe. Wine funds may not be best for the risk-averse, though, since a dropped bottle or a power outage at a storage facility can quickly destroy an investment's value.

Art snobs. Art can be an asset class, too, and stats show auctioned art can reap tremendous gains. That is, if you're a high roller, which hope-fully you someday will be. The Mei/Moses Fine Art Index tracks roughly nine thousand repeat art sales using auction records dating back to 1875. The cofounder of the fund told me his research shows art has a similar long-term return to stocks, but it's more risky.

Race-car fans. The StockCar Stocks Index (ticker: SCARX) requires a $250 minimum investment and offers a broad portfolio of stocks linked to NASCAR, including its sponsors. Stocks in the fund include dependable blue chip names like Exxon Mobil. Since its launch in 1998 until 2006, SCARX returned about 8 percent annually.

And now I pass on the torch to Jim Cramer, who has taught me so much about the fundamentals. I never thought I would be one to get giddy over stocks, but Jim makes this stuff so accessible and exciting, you can't help but want to learn more.

HOW STOCK SPECULATING CAN MAKE YOU RICH

James J. Cramer

Between 1978 and 1979, I saved and put $1,500 toward my retirement. This, while living in my car for much of the year, but that's another story. I let that money sit in a Fidelity account, and thanks to compound interest, most people could live on that amount for at least a few years in retirement. But the return is nowhere near where it could have been had I invested that money in the stock market. I was too conservative in my twenties. And that's my biggest gripe today: Too many young folks are being way too conservative. I'm here to tell you now, don't be one of them, at least not if you ever want to enjoy having the big bucks.

That's because having more money is not just a luxury, it's a necessity if you have any plans of getting "ahead" in life, be it to pay off your student loans, have enough disposable income to buy more stuff, or earn what you need for a comfortable retirement. You have to be aggressive. You have to make your money grow quickly. There's no other way to get ahead, unless of course you win the tristate lotto.

The truth is, every penny you leave in a bank account with an interest rate that at best outpaces inflation by a percentage point or two is little more than a penny wasted. I'd still recommend a savings account over spending that dough, but if you're looking to ensure your financial freedom, choosing savings over stocks—especially while you're young—is about as irresponsible as pouring your money down the drain.

Now I know, stocks are risky and a bank account is anything but. But I say so what? Risk is the price of upside, and now is the best time in your life to take chances. I cannot stress how critical it is to be speculative and take risks today because even if you get shred to tiny, little, shriveled-up pieces in the market, you have your entire life to win it back. Think about it: Compound interest means the money you invest when you're twenty-five is essentially worth more than what you invest at thirty-five, because it has more time to grow. The unfortunate flipside here is that whatever you don't invest while you're still young costs a lot more over the long run than money you don't invest when you're a decade or two older. The number one strategy for you: Be aggressive. Stock up on speculative stocks, in addition to high-growth equities, either through mutual funds or through your own stock picks, until you're well into your thirties. (That also means you shouldn't own any bonds.) Farnoosh covers the basics on stock picking and investing for retirement, so I'm going to leave those to her and tell you about my favorite kind of investing and the best way to make money when you're young: speculative stocks.

High-risk speculative stocks have given me my biggest wins. How big are we talking here? With the gains from just one trade, a bet that Chevron's bid for Gulf Oil would succeed even though the street thought it would be blocked by the regulators, I made enough money to pay for all three years of law school while I was still in it. The trade was reckless beyond belief, since I threw all of my money into Gulf Oil call options, but the gamble paid off handsomely. I would still never recommend that anyone, no matter how young, put all his or her money in one stock, let alone options, because those options could have easily gone to zero in minutes if I'd been wrong. It doesn't get any worse than losing all of your money. But if you take a step back and look at the downside in the context of my entire life, it becomes less significant. Being broke in law school is a walk in the park compared to being broke when you've got a family to support or your retirement to pay for. More generally, losing money in the market when you're young hurts a lot less than losing it later in life. Plus, if you're smarter than I was and diversify your holdings, you won't lose all your money anyway, even when you take a big gamble with some of it. And that's why I recommend taking some chances. As long as you follow the basic ground rules when it comes to stocks and speculate wisely, you're much more likely to win than lose. This is the part of your life where it pays to take big risks on stocks, in part because the gains can be enormous but mostly because your losses will matter less than they will at any other point in your life to come.

➤ ➤ ➤ ➤ Cramer's Ground Rules for Investors

Care. Do you care about the world of business, how companies make money and how much potential they have to make more money? Bottom line: You shouldn't invest in the stock market if you have zero inclinations. You have to have the hunger. I've always believed that you need to dedicate the same amount of time to monitor your stock picks as to keep tabs on your favorite sports team. Would you rush to check your stock as fast as you rush to watch *Lost* or *24* or the Eagles game? If the answer is yes, then by all means, keep reading. (Go, Eagles!)

Make time. The market is too intense. You need at least one hour per week per stock to stay on top of your investments. In that hour, you need to be up on the latest publicly available information you can get your hands on related to your stock. That includes news articles about your stock and its industry peers (though use your judgment and be thorough in your news clippings; you can't believe everything you read). Closely examine analyst reports, Securities and Exchange Commission filings, and quarterly conference calls and earnings reports from the company. Remember, when a company reports its financial results, it typically holds a conference call for everyone, including institutional investors, analysts, and shareholders (you). It's mandatory for them, and it should be mandatory for you, as an investor, to listen in with a critical ear. It's all available and downloadable off the company's or SEC's Web site. Thestreet.com is also packed with brilliant and investable ideas, as well as deep analysis that can help guide your investment choices. It's all at your fingertips for free. No excuses!

Have money. You need money to invest money. There's no way around that, unfortunately. Considering a minimum of five stocks, I've always said you need at least $2,500 to begin. That's about $500 per stock. Don't have that kind of money? Start figuring out how you can get it. Look, that might mean using your Christmas bonus one year to open an account or maybe you'll get that initial money back from a tax return. I know it's hard enough at your stage in life to have a few thousand saved, but hey, maybe you're going to have to say good-bye to your well-preserved 1980s action figures on eBay. Maybe you have to babysit your older brother's four-year-old twins every Friday night for a year to accumulate some investment dollars. Again, this speaks to my first rule, which is, you must care. You must be passionate. If there's a will, you'll find a way to get into the market.

Have a second opinion. Before you hop onto your online brokerage site to make a trade, make sure you've considered a second opinion from a friend or experienced investor. This doesn't have to be a fancy broker you pay through the nose for. Have someone you can at least bounce an idea off of.

This ain't your father's investment portfolio. You need to live a little more dangerously, so to speak. That's right, when you're young, the name of the game is speculation. To some, including the vast majority of people who write about stocks, speculation is a dirty word and a foolish practice. To me it's an essential element of good investing and a source of major gains if you know what you're doing. I've said in the past that no more than 20 percent of a diversified portfolio should be in speculative stocks, but in your twenties it wouldn't be crazy to speculate with half of your portfolio. (Note: We're talking nonretirement money here. With your retirement stocks you should take a more conservative approach.)

So how the heck do you make smart, lucrative speculations? First, you look for a stock that can hit a grand slam, even though you recognize that should things go wrong, it will strikeout. My rule of thumb is that if you pick five promising speculative stocks, three will do next-to-nothing, one will go to zero, and the last one will go so much higher that your five-stock speculative portfolio turns a sizable profit, justifying the whole endeavor. In this way, speculation is responsible for my biggest wins and worst losses. In my charitable trust, which you can see at www.actionalertsplus .com, a subscription service where I explain every trade I make to readers, my worst loss was in the speculative stock, Charter Communications (ticker: CHTR), a beaten-down cable company that was trading at around $4 when I started buying it. By the way, never assume that a stock won't go a lot lower just because it's already been knocked down into the single digits.

➤ ➤ ➤ ➤ How to Pick Speculative Stocks

Price point. Look for stocks under $10, meaning their share price is in the single digits. The actual share price isn't supposed to tell you anything about a stock in theory, but in fact, it tends to reveal a great deal about a company. You won't catch a CEO celebrating when the stock he's responsible for joins the under-$10 cohort. This is a space that's filled with the stocks of companies that have failed, blundered, or simply been unable to draw the attention of or create enthusiasm on Wall Street. In other words, many speculative stocks are tied to companies that have a history of doing poorly. (That's why they're risky.)

Market capitalizations. Most companies with a market capitalization of under a billion dollars, and all companies with market caps of less than $500 million, should be treated as speculative.

Profit. When a young company has yet to turn a profit, its stock is almost certainly speculative. You'll see this often in biotech firms—if they have little earnings and their stocks trade mostly on news about products, almost always drugs in development, they're speculative.

Analyst coverage. Stocks of fairly small companies, think those with market caps under three or four billion dollars, that have very little analyst coverage—no more than two analysts on the stock—are speculative. I call these orphans and wear a red Little Orphan Annie wig when I discuss these on my television show *Mad Money*. One of the great things about stocks with little coverage is that in sharp contrast to large-cap names with a dozen analysts watching their every move, there's a real dearth of information on under-covered speculative stocks. That can give you a big edge if you follow the stock closely, because others won't when information isn't easily available.

When I talk about speculation, it's important to understand that I'm not giving you a license to gamble. As a young investor, you should take risks, true, but they need to be *calculated* risks on stocks that you understand. To be honest, the worst gamblers in the market are the investors who have been seduced by the buy and hold mentality. I always say I believe in buy and homework, not buy and hold. The ideology of buy and hold says that you should find high-quality stocks and own them for years and years. Buy and hold is popular, it's easy, and it's convinced far too many people that it's a responsible long-term strategy—long-term because when you buy and hold you don't have to pay attention to distracting short-term items like news and your stock's performance. I think buying a stock and then trusting it to go higher for the next five years without doing any research to make sure things are working out the way you'd hoped is the definition of gambling in the stock market.

Instead, I advocate buying and doing an hour of research per week on every stock you own to make sure they're still worth owning—and dumping them if they're not. Smart speculators always do the homework, even if it sounds suspiciously like high school to the ears of someone who graduated from it not that long ago. But maybe you would have had more incentive to do those algebra problems if they could have made you rich.

Here's your first assignment: Develop a thesis—a reason or reasons why you believe your speculative stock will go higher. You should do this for all stocks, but it's especially important to speculating. Once you have a thesis, you'll want to test it as rigorously as possible. For instance, if you have a good reason to expect that a company will do something to cause more investors to buy its stock and send the share price higher, look at how other companies or the company you like have done after doing the same thing or something similar. If you like a speculative stock because you believe it will announce better-than-expected earnings, you can look around and see that most companies that beat earnings estimates see their stocks move higher afterward. That's an obvious example but true nevertheless.

Then make sure that your thesis isn't already baked into the stock, meaning that the share price doesn't already reflect what you expect to happen. This is more guesswork, but your guess should still be educated. Be sure also to weigh your thesis against any likely events that might push your speculative stock lower. You don't want to buy a stock, turn out to be right, and still lose money because something you didn't spend enough time thinking about drives the stock lower anyway. I've seen a lot of regular people who are right-on when it comes to what they like about an individual company buy that company's stock and get crushed because of problems with the sector their stock belongs to. Always keep the bigger picture in mind: Half of a stock's movement is determined by the performance of its sector, the kind of business it's in.

One secret to success when it comes to speculating is a healthy dose of cynicism. To put it bluntly, you're not looking for a stock that you believe will be able to produce terrific earnings in four or five years when you speculate; you're looking for a stock that has the ability to convince others it will have those great earnings in four or five years. You want a stock that's on its way to being popular and sexy, but it's not quite there yet. That means figuring out if a company has the kind of story that it can sell to Wall Street, because once its sector comes into favor, the speculative stocks that might have seemed like the worst of breed players in the industry will often outperform the stocks that are the best of breed because the street had much lower expectations for them.

Another thing that gives oomph to the speculative stocks in a sector that's really on fire is that investors who made money in the sector's higher-quality stocks will look around for other stocks that haven't moved nearly as much as the best of breed stocks. Invariably they'll find the little, poorly performing spec stock and buy it hand over fist.

The speculative names that trade under $10 are especially good at riding a rising tide in their sector because it doesn't take much to push a stock trading in the single digits higher. In other words, you don't buy the worst company in an industry because you think it's terrific, you buy it when the industry is doing well and right before the high-quality stocks start running out of steam. It's risky because you're buying a stock with a lot of problems, but these will often do well if they're part of a strong sector. And remember, if you're looking to spot the next sexy stock or group of stocks, you shouldn't speculate with a stock that entrances you unless it also happens to be the one that you think will entrance the street.

Timing is also important when speculating. You need to recognize a soon-to-be-sexy stock earlier than most, so sometimes it's better to take a pass than to bet too late. My favorite metaphor for the market is that Wall Street is a big fashion show and stocks come in and out of favor just like styles of clothing. It's not always easy to tell what style will be in next season, but a season is a long time, and once you've seen the stocks that are in, they stay in for a while even if they're fashionable for the wrong reasons. When we speculate, we don't care if the street is right or wrong to embrace the stocks that are in, what we care about is knowing what's in style and knowing when to get out of a group that's losing its sizzle.

A great illustration of this point is Dendreon (ticker: DNDN), a small biotech company that has had a lot of true believers and a lot of people who absolutely hate its stock and short it viciously or borrow shares to sell with the idea the price would fall. Remember, when it comes to speculating, you don't want to be a true believer, but you don't want to hate the stock passionately either. Dendreon's prostate cancer drug called Provenge, which I often have pretended to confuse with Provasic, the drug from *The Fugitive*, received the endorsement of an important FDA panel shortly before the FDA was scheduled to decide whether to approve the drug. This sent the stock flying from a closing price of $5.22 on March 28, to open at $17.92 on March 30 after trading in it was suspended for a day because of the news. The stock then traded between $12 and $15 for the next week and a half until it jumped again and peaked at $25.25 on April 10. But the FDA didn't approve Provenge, and by May 9 Dendreon's stock was back in the single digits.

The moral of the story is twofold. If you were a true believer in Dendreon, you likely held on for too long and gave back your enormous gain (although if you follow my advice about taking profits in a stock, you would have sold most of your shares after both the large moves, because discipline—like selling at least half of your position when you catch a double—always trumps conviction). However, if you took Dendreon too seriously and hated the stock, you either missed a major opportunity to make money or you spent over a month in a very tough position if you were one of the shorts. A cynical speculator would have bought the stock after the FDA panel's recommendation, which was what I recommended on *Mad Money,* not because our cynic thought the drug would be approved by the FDA, but because he thought Dendreon's true believers would be willing to buy even more stock and be able to win more converts.

You're probably starting to see that there's a life cycle to speculative stocks, and it's relatively short. That's another reason not to become too emotionally involved with a company. It gets much harder to recognize where you are in the life cycle and get out with a big profit while it's still there. In the Dendreon example that would have meant selling before the FDA announced its decision on the drug. Dendreon's success was especially short lived, but generally speaking, when you've already made money in a speculative play and there's a catalyst coming that could take away your profits and then some, it doesn't pay to wait around for the extra upside. The worst that happens is that you get out of the stock with a profit before it goes even higher, and I guarantee you that's better than any scenario where you lose money, the potential downside if you don't sell.

➤ ➤ ➤ ➤ **When to Bail on Speculative Stocks**

How do you know when to get out after a large gain? Often you'll be dealing with a stock that went from having little to no analyst coverage on the street to one with a ballooning number of analysts issuing buy recommendations. At a certain point, usually once there are four or five analysts from the major brokers covering the stock, it becomes overexposed, everyone now knows about it, and all the investors who want to buy have already bought. Selling when you get four analysts from the big investment banks on the stock is a good rule of thumb. Another telltale sign is when a piece of good news comes out and the stock doesn't go any higher. With a speculative name you sell because it's another sign that demand has dried up, and demand is all that powers these things.

You have an incredible opportunity to speculate while you're in your twenties, and you're young enough to lose money, even a lot of money, in the market without screwing up your future. And it can also give you spectacular gains that sure beat living out of your car to save money. Speculation, more than any other part of investing, can be thrilling and fun. But don't take my word for it. Go buy some speculative stocks and see for yourself.

CHAPTER 8

HOMEWARD BOUND

"Rent is just money down the drain." —You, me, everyone

How many times have you said that? And sensed you didn't have any other choice? Feel like all the folks who own a house earn way more money than you, are married with two-and-a-half kids, and never go out on the weekends? Well, true, the nuclear family does make up a significant portion of the country's home owners. In fact, married couples make up more than 60 percent of all home purchases, according to the National Association of Realtors. But what if we look at a home as an *investment* vehicle instead of a place to own once you get hitched and have babies? Buying a house is one surefire way (in the long term) to make money with money and to have your hard-earned money grow at a faster rate than the snail pace your local bank is offering. You can build some serious equity. How does an average 10 to 12 percent annual appreciation sound to you? Do I have your attention yet?

The reality is, you *do* have a choice. It is possible to become a home owner before the gray hairs arrive. And while the market goes up and down and some years prove more robust than others for real estate, buying a home is hands-down one of the best long-term personal investments. Not to mention, a home offers the *survival* benefit of a roof over your head. You just can't beat it.

Remember Anna's ridiculously cheap apartment, the one with the cat I told you about in chapter 2? All the astonishing features of the living situation—and there were more than a few!—were quickly trumped by the fact that Anna had been living there for more than twenty years! So add to the fact that she had been renting since the 1970s and had zero equity in her home, she had little in savings. She was still borrowing money from her parents, who had advised her to buy property fifteen years earlier. They'd even offered to help! But she thought her rent was too good to pass up. I suppose Anna's financial situation could be summarized in one story: We had a twice-monthly house cleaner for whom we split the cost. One morning I ran out of the house to catch a class without leaving my half on the living room table. Anna kindly covered my half, and when I paid her back that evening, she asked for an extra $1. Turns out Anna had to run to the ATM machine to pay the full amount and thought, since she was covering for me, I should also pay half the ATM surcharge. (Did I mention she was in her late forties and had a law degree?)

And then I did the math. How much money had Anna paid in rent, approximately, over those twenty years? Assuming her monthly charge started somewhere in the $700s and ended at $1,500 over the course of two decades, my math puts that at $264,000 down the toilet.

Instead, take note of our peer Theresa. She's the perfect case study for what has become the fastest-growing group of home buyers in the United States: single women. In 2006, they accounted for 22 percent of recent home purchases. Single men accounted for 9 percent of purchases. Theresa's story basically tells me that young, single professionals can and should invest in real estate. Heck, even I did it, earning a little more than $46,000 a year and living in too-hot-to-handle Manhattan, where the average apartment goes for $1.3 million (at last check). Crazy things can happen.

HAPPY HOME OWNER: THERESA

Age: twenty-six
Occupation: ceramics engineer
From: upstate New York
Adores: softball and discount racks

Upon graduation, my friend Theresa was living in Pleasanton, California, earning $50,000 a year as a ceramics engineer and spending $600 a month on rent with a roommate. When she later got transferred to North Carolina, she realized how much further her dollar could stretch in that area. By financing a $134,000 home, her mortgage would equal her former rent.

Theresa's First Home. "I had no idea what I was doing," Theresa admits. "My mom is a paralegal at a law office that does real estate so she gave me pointers." Theresa looked at thirty houses in two days, as her company was looking to immediately relocate her from California (her company paid for the broker fees).

She finally settled on a 1,400-square-foot house in Winston-Salem with three bedrooms, two bathrooms, a game room, cathedral ceilings, a Jacuzzi, and a small patio. Price: $134,000.

How Did She Afford It? She's wicked disciplined. "The biggest thing that's helped me is that ever since I started my career, I always put twenty-five to thirty percent of my salary in a 'don't touch it' account for a 'big purchase' down the road." One year she had saved up enough to contribute a $15,000 lump sum toward her student loan. Another year she paid the 20 percent down payment on her home in North Carolina. That was a personal goal of hers, knowing she didn't want to carry too much weight on her shoulders for a home. She says, "When I was little, my parents took us to the pumpkin patch and told us, 'You can only get the pumpkin you can carry.'"

Her Second Place. After about a year, Theresa's company relocated her to Loveland, Colorado, where she, again, decided to purchase a home. This time, she had earned some equity ($4,000) in her first home and had put away some additional savings, not to mention she had a higher salary. Her 2,400-square-foot house boasts berber carpeting, shiny hardwood, tile kitchen, crown moldings, and a big ol' deck that seats three Adirondack chairs. This place has three bedrooms, too. Price tag: $206,000.

How Did She Pay for It? She put down 40 percent and borrowed $166,000 from the bank with a five-year adjustable-rate mortgage. Her loan payment is $900 a month. "I was going to do a seven-year adjustable-rate mortgage, but I wasn't sure I would be living there that long," she says.

Theresa's Good Life. To continue owning a home, to have enough money to travel back home to Upstate New York to visit family and friends a few times a year. "I don't sacrifice time with my family." Theresa's big passion is skiing and she has an all-season pass to a mountain near her home in Colorado. She also is a big organic food lover, never hesitating to pay $5 for raspberries. As for the future, she foresees marriage and kids. But before that time arrives, she'd like to have already moved back to the East Coast to be closer to her parents and relatives.

What's Not in Her Equation. "I don't waste money on clothing. I have a full closet, but I will rarely buy anything unless it's on the sale rack. . . . In the last six months, I don't remember something I spent more than fifteen dollars on." Theresa also hasn't had a car payment since 1999. She's been driving around her 1995 Ford Escort because a newer vehicle just wasn't a priority. Oh yeah, and she doesn't go to the movies. She waits for the DVDs.

Theresa's Tip for Starter Single-Home Buyers. Don't buy something really, really old, unless you have the money to spend on reconstruction, maintenance, and upkeep. To calm her parents' worries and her own nervousness about being a single home owner for the first time at the young age of twenty-two, Theresa bought a brandnew house that didn't require fixing up or maintenance. The home also came with a one-year warranty because it was brand-spanking new. "I didn't have the fear of things going wrong," she says.

➤ ➤ ➤ ➤ ➤ **Broker Feedback**

I've known Kathy Braddock for almost four years. She is one of New York's premier real-estate experts and runs her own consulting firm, braddock+purcell in Manhattan. She works in the country's hottest real-estate market, but her tips for first-time buyers are really practical and applicable in all parts of the United States. I used her advice when buying my own apartment in Manhattan in 2004. Here's the Q&A she asks of all young buyers.

How long do you think you will be in your first home? That means thinking long and hard as to your career and social paths. If you think that you will be here less than three years, don't buy, she says. It is too short a period of time and you might end up losing money. The exception is that if you do move before three years but can afford to keep your home while renting it out, it may make sense to buy.

What can you afford? Speak with a couple of mortgage brokers or bankers and get prequalified for a mortgage, which no matter who tells you what, is free! Most of the time you will be qualified for more than you really want to spend. In this case, remember Theresa's pumpkin-patch story. The general rule of thumb is you don't want to take on a mortgage that's more than 2.5 times your annual salary.

What do you know? In other words, have you done your research? Read the real-estate section of your local paper religiously. Scour Craigslist. Get a sense of how much homes are costing in your desired neighborhood. While there is soo much on the Web, a real-estate agent, a *good* one, can be extremely helpful. I'll define *good* in a separate sidebar. There are a lot of stinky real-estate agents who end up being a waste of your time.

How bad do you want the place? Never want a place so badly that you can't see beyond the fog of love. Take away the emotion. There will always be another home, just like all those fish in the sea, Kathy tells me.

➤ ➤ ➤ ➤ **Interviewing a Real-Estate Broker**

Kathy also suggests being very thorough as you interview real-estate brokers (whether you're in the market to buy or rent). Remember, the seller pays the commission so you won't necessarily save money by going it alone. As for how to find real-estate agents, ask for referrals from friends and family who've bought homes in the neighborhood(s) that interest you. Interview with at least three agents. Be concerned if the agent . . .

... calls everything "fabulous!" all the time. You want someone who is dead honest, someone who has a range of opinions and who really gets what it is you are looking for, not someone who has his or her own agenda.

... just got licensed. You want someone with at least a few years of experience.

... is not familiar with the neighborhood. The point of hiring an agent is to team up with someone with more knowledge of real estate and residential neighborhoods than you have. Ask how long the agent has sold homes in the area. Ask for his or her track record in the neighborhood. If the agent doesn't give it to you, walk away.

... only works on the weekends. Licensed real-estate brokers were a dime a dozen in the early 2000s when everyone's home was tripling overnight. In 2004 in New York, at least, it was the most popular license exam, following the bar. With everyone and their German shepherd getting licensed, many of those folks worked a separate full-time job. For your first home purchase, especially, you want someone who is completely dedicated to your hunt, someone you can call on a Wednesday afternoon or Friday morning with questions or concerns.

HAPPY HOME OWNER: FARNOOSH

Age: twenty-eight
Hometown: Worcester, Massachusetts
Schooling: Penn State and Columbia
Guilty pleasures: dark chocolate–peanut M&Ms and Justin Timberlake

How Farnoosh Bought Her Apartment in Manhattan at Twenty-four

January 2004. I was still living in the apartment with Anna. I was working at New York 1 News as a business news producer. My salary: $46,600 a year. My rent, meantime, was a hard-to-beat $500 a month. I knew I couldn't live there *forever* since the cat was driving me nuts (as were Anna's cheapskate ways). But with my so-so salary, it was close to impossible to find an equally spacious and safe apartment in Manhattan for so little. I figured I could afford $1,100 a month at most, but even that wasn't going to cut it—not unless I wanted to live with three or four other people.

What to do? I wanted to move but couldn't afford much and didn't want to make major living concessions. "What about buying a place?" my father asked one day. Um, well, for starters I wasn't making enough money, especially with property in Manhattan averaging more than $1 million a unit. And by "average unit" I mean a 750-square-foot apartment with two bedrooms (fourth-floor walk-up).

At the time, all I could dream of affording was a small studio apartment, sized 350 to 400 square feet. Those were going for a cool $250,000 to $350,000, depending on the neighborhood and building type. Translation: Forget about it.

It was my father who ultimately planted the ingenious seed in my brain, convincing me that I *should* consider buying an apartment. After all, I was never, ever planning on leaving this amazing city. My job and livelihood depended on it.

In the end, my dad encouraged me to look at apartments between $250K and $300K, repeating that he had "a plan." So, intrigued by my dad's "plan," I started seeing four or five apartments a weekend, all without a broker, meaning I generally saw apartments being sold by the owner. I probably missed out on some hidden deals as a result. You have to also remember that this was 2004, when real estate was nearing its hot, hot, hotness in Manhattan, when owners didn't feel the need to hire brokers since their apartments were likely to encounter bidding wars no matter what.

My Search. I looked at about a dozen places and nothing looked livable. Every studio looked like a dorm room, with the bed the first thing you see when you walk in. I couldn't believe one-room apartments in Manhattan were selling for more than three-, four-, and five-bedroom homes elsewhere. I settled on my current apartment because (1) it was in a safe neighborhood, (2) it had a doorman and an elevator, and (3) it was a condo, which meant no crazy board approval process. Also, the monthly maintenance fees were relatively inexpensive.

How I Financed It. My parents used their home equity line of credit to completely pay for the apartment. Two days later I went to Washington Mutual and got a personal line of credit worth 80 percent of the appraised value of my apartment (which was actually more than the purchase price). With that money, I immediately wrote a check to my parents to help pay them back. After I sell the place, I plan to give them 20 percent of what I earn. To them, it's like storing money in an asset that's already appreciated almost 100 percent in four years. (Editor's note: Lines of credit on a home are based on the current appraisal value, not how much you paid.)

TAKEAWAY 1: ASK RELATIVES FOR FINANCIAL HELP

I admit: I was darn lucky. My parents had the foresight and the equity in their existing home to go in on this apartment with me. Parents aren't the only ones who may be interested in getting a slice of a real-estate deal. In all seriousness, most family members' homes have appreciated a fair amount over the years. (Around the beginning of 2006, the housing market in the United States started to crumble, but long-term home owners have probably still acquired some substantial equity.) Like my parents, they may be able to take equity out of their home and give it to you as a down payment. "With interest rates as low as they are, it will not cost them very much extra in monthly payments. And if they have no mortgage or a small one, then they can deduct that interest," says Kathy Braddock. "Or they might be able to take out a home equity loan, as opposed to refinancing." Bottom line, without tapping into their stocks or bank accounts, they might be able to help you with very little sacrifice.

TAKEAWAY 2: YOU CAN AFFORD IT ON YOUR OWN

While the days of subprime mortgages and advertisements for 0 percent down, interest-only loans are few and far between due to all the recent defaults, some banks still offer attractive financing deals that don't require a down payment to credit-worthy borrowers. First things first, you want to make sure your credit report is 100 percent accurate and in shipshape condition. Next, get preapproved for a mortgage by contacting your local bank or brokerage. Never, ever take on a mortgage product that seems too good to be true. Look at the length and projected payouts of the loan and make sure that you can afford it in the years to come.

FOOLPROOF FURNITURE SHOPPING

Your place may be small, but it can be pretty expensive filling it up with furniture. While the aisles of IKEA and Target are chock-full of first-time home furnishings, know that sometimes cheap doesn't mean "worth it," which doesn't mean "smart." Just like with cars and electronics, you can go really wrong with a coffee table or a couch. And if you do, you're way worse off in furniture land than in the world of cars or electronics. Why? This $78 billion furniture market is unregulated. In fact, in 2002, the government lifted all restrictions for furniture retailers to appropriately label pieces. So, to better prepare you for your next furniture spree, consider these tips and lesser-known facts.

First, Scour the Web. Most times the Web offers better sales and deals on furniture, according to retail experts, and people are catching on. "Sixty percent shop online today before going into a store," says Jennifer Litwin, industry watchdog and author of *Furniture Hot Spots* and *Best Furniture Buying Tips Ever!* But the Web shouldn't be the only place to search. If you're not sure about an item's listing online, visit the related store to see it in person. Sometimes that's hard to do, for example if you're buying an item online with no physical store nearby. But beware that even while the photo on the Web looks spectacular, it's never the best way to examine the true color and texture. For one thing, you can't see the finish.

Ransack the Store. Go at it. When you shop locally, enter the furniture showroom with a critical eye for spotting lemons. Avoid couches and chairs that have staples and screws that can fall out easily. Instead, look for items made with stitching and wielding. Turn over cushions! Look under tabletops! Pull out drawers!

Size It Up. Know not just what's going to fit in your home, but also what will fit through your front door. Take floor and ceiling measurements and write down the dimensions of doors, hall-ways, and elevators to make sure certain furniture can be properly delivered.

Get a Written Warranty. If the store doesn't already provide one, ask for a written warranty and a description of how you can return goods and under what conditions. "Ask the store to put the materials in writing," Litwin says. "Many stores incorrectly de-scribe or label their pieces." And read the fine print: Sometimes the return policy includes a restocking fee.

Ask for a Discount or Free Delivery. Remember, it never hurts to ask for freebies when you're buying a big-ticket item. Ask for a 15 percent discount when shopping at a local retailer, the same discount designers generally get.

Don't Settle for Subpar. If your piece of furniture arrives scratched up, bent, or irregular in any way, shape, or form, or if it is missing a piece or two, know that you're not obligated to keep it, and that means you're not required to pay for the item. But this is something you must act on immediately. Don't wait for the de-livery person to leave. You need a witness to see that the item ar-rived knocked up.

Warm Up Your Wrench. I'll never forget when I ordered a couch from www.target.com and it arrived in boxes. I literally had to as-semble a microfiber, wood-based couch. But that's how it works these days; 65 percent of furniture needs to be assembled upon ar-rival. Bear in mind that this may cost you time and money (and a sore back).

➤ ➤ ➤ ➤ ➤ Small Quarters, Lotsa Room

My apartment is 400 square feet—about four times the size of your average Starbucks' restroom. In New York City it's nothing to complain about, but space does get tight. How to make your small quarters functional so you can eat, sleep, bathe, and do yoga all without breaking lamps and tripping over your own feet? (And for the record, I've fit more than twelve people comfortably into my apartment for costume parties and holiday merrying. I think that's pretty impressive.)

Multipurpose. For $500, my JC Penney queen-size bed functions as both a beauty-sleeping device and, thanks to its six built-in bottom baskets, a secret place to store my winter sweaters and extra sheets. My point: Buy double-purpose furniture. Something as simple as a stepladder, for example, can also be used to display plants or picture frames. *Incidentally, my JC Penney bed cost a quarter the price of a strikingly similar bed at Pottery Barn. I mean reaallly similar.*

Sleeper Sofa It. Before I had my giant bed, I had a sleeper sofa. It was awesome for a couple of years because it made my apartment more inviting for guests. But to be honest, it eventually became a pain in the back and neck. The truth is, I hardly ever rolled the bed out. Instead, I would crash on the couch—which is no way to sleep. Sleeper sofas or futons can be a cheaper, space-friendly way to furnish your small home, but I don't recommend making it a way of life. Just do it temporarily, or it could end up costing you big bucks in chiropractic visits.

Divide and conquer. My friend Jessica paid $1,000 to put up a wall in what was her one-bedroom apartment and turned it into a two bedroom, which in turn became extra revenue for her, as she took on a roommate. Check with your landlord to make sure this is permissible.

➤ ➤ ➤ ➤ Trash Picking 101: Still Another Way to Get Furniture for Less

I asked my friend Ben, who works on Jim Cramer's *Mad Money* show on CNBC, if he had any tips for my book, some invaluable advice that gets him to live beyond his means without spending a lot of money. His response: "One of my favorite pastimes on the weekend is getting in my car and driving around the neighborhood. You never know what you'll find by the curbside." Ben's rescued from the street a box spring, a bed frame, an end table, three beach chairs, an umbrella, an ironing board, and a bookshelf. That's an easy $500 saved. I asked him to elaborate.

Basic ground rules. "One must wade carefully in the waters of trash-pickery," warns Ben. First and foremost, he says, avoid all things edible. (Duh!) Next, make sure the items are, indeed, left for trash pickup. He says it's safest to go trash shopping after the sun sets. And if anyone asks where you got the item? "Tell them you got it at a yard sale."

But, I never find useful trash! No worries, says Ben. Perhaps you are from a small town filled with pack rats or live in a yard sale–intense town. If used consumer items are not making their way to sidewalks near you, drive to your state capital, says Ben, or a city where space is at a premium and time is at a minimum (like New York, Boston, Chicago).

HAPPY HOME OWNER: FARON

Age: twenty-seven
Hometown: "Allentown, P.A., baby!"
Current locale: Philly suburb
Schooling: Penn State

Degree: B.S. in management information systems
Occupation: energy trading consultant
Loathes: clowns
Favorite cocktail: black Russian

How He Financed His First Home. His main "sacrifices," as he calls them (I prefer to say "alternate living choices"), were living at home with his parents in Allentown for a year and a half after school and commuting to work fifty-five miles each way. "At least I didn't have a curfew!"

Also. Faron says he adhered relatively well to his "good life" equation, faithfully using Quicken (did I mention he's a techie?) to manage all his expenses. He also invested money set aside from birthdays, his Bar Mitzvah, and the piggy bank from his childhood.

What He Bought. A sixty-year-old, two-story brick colonial in a Philadelphia suburb. It has three bedrooms, one bathroom, a finished basement, and a sunroom.

The Most Traumatic Part. "You are so at the whim of the people representing you that it's disconcerting, and I didn't like the lack of control or insight into the process."

What He Wished He Had Known Ahead of Time. Never go with a real-estate agent who you don't have references for if you can avoid it. Even though his initial Realtor came recommended by a coworker, Faron discovered the hard way that the two of them didn't quite match in the personality department. "Clearly and plainly state your expectations of them upfront. I like direct and frequent communication, and she seemed to lack both."

"I replaced that Realtor with another indirect referral who seemed to meet my new criteria—someone like my Jewish mother but even more of a bulldog." He also cautions to avoid paying any sort of fee to brokers as a buyer. "If they charge fees, be sure they're consistent with the practices in the industry." Next, he adds, when you start looking for a house, ask for a sample close sheet upfront.

Surviving the Close. The close process was painful, he described, due to the number of papers you have to sign and the amount of money you have to part with. "People rarely spend the time to read everything, and those of us who do tend to find ourselves overwhelmed with the fine print. In my case, I read through everything and found two errors that, while minor, had to be amended and initialed by the mortgage company prior to the close ending. You never know what could be wrong and result in financial misfortunes for the buyer. Caveat emptor."

Why Faron Chose a Fixer-Upper. Cost. "I saved about thirty-five K in the asking price compared to similar houses in the neighborhood, as a result. I was willing to apply my rudimentary carpentry skills to the project (what Realtors so lovingly refer to as 'sweat equity') and sacrifice down-payment money for improvement equity." Faron says he feels as though he built substantial equity in the home while greatly improving its attractiveness and amenities. "My hope is that the cash I used to improve the house will actually do so at a rate of seventy-five to a hundred and fifty percent, so that I'd have a good ROI [return on investment] in terms of home value." Faron is what you call "a numbers guy."

Financing the Deal. Faron put down 5 percent, financed 80 percent with a thirty-year fixed mortgage, and financed the remaining 15 percent with a fixed-rate home equity loan. This is called a piggy-back fixed home equity loan.

Faron's Advice for First-Time Buyers. Stay informed about your investment, he says. "Read up on the things that make the house work and function so that when they go wrong (and believe me—everything goes wrong), you're at least somewhat knowledgeable about them." Additionally, he urges you stay on top of the market in your city, the country at large, and especially your immediate neighborhood. Sale prices are a matter of public record, so you should make it your business every six months or so to see what homes in your area sold for, and whenever you see a house go up for sale, go online and see what the seller is asking for it. This way, you have an approximate understanding of the value of your home and, thus, your equity.

HAPPY HOME OWNER: KATHY

Age: twenty-eight
Current locale: New Jersey
Schooling: New York University
Occupation: Web site news producer
Favorite TV show: *Grey's Anatomy*
What she's dying to buy if she just had enough money: Lexus IS 250
Student loans upon graduation: none
Credit-card debt: none

Kathy's Key to Early Home Ownership. Living at home in New Jersey with her parents after college. "Right out of NYU, I was doing pretty well for a twenty-two-year-old. I continued working at the radio station where I had worked throughout college," she says. "I pocketed all the money I made, which was decent thanks to being in a union and working overnight shifts at times or early mornings where a nighttime differential kicked in (overnights basically meant double pay.)" Six months after graduating and living with Mom and Dad, she moved to South Carolina to work at a local TV station, where the pay was "terrible," or $20,000 a year, but the experience would be worth it. A year later she was right back in New York City, working as a producer for a local TV station, earning $50,000 a year—more than double! "Things got significantly better for me in my third (and current) job." She continued to work while living at her parents' home. "All I paid for were things like my cell phone, car insurance, gasoline . . . but no rent or mortgage or any household bills. By living at home for about four years I saved about fifty thousand."

Why Buy in New Jersey? As much as Kathy adores New York City, she decided to pass on the idea of renting a teeny-tiny apartment on the fourth floor of a walk-up building. New Jersey offers her the convenience of proximity and cheaper living. "It takes five minutes to get to the Lincoln Tunnel from my new home."

The Hunt. Kathy scoured the Internet for apartments (mostly Craigslist) and got free advice from her father, a former banker, as well as her brother, a credit analyst, about how much she could realistically afford. "I learned two very important things. . . . First, that your home shouldn't cost more than 2.5 times your salary and second, your home is equity so even if you put a lot of money into it, you're getting it back when you sell (usually)."

Preparing to Close. Kathy says be patient. It took her about three months to finalize all the paperwork. Also, she purchased a co-op, which means board approval, which means more wait time.

How Her Parents Helped. Kathy's parents didn't help her pay for the co-op, per se, although she did pay her down payment by cashing in on the stocks her dad had given her while she was growing up. They also offered her a second opinion on the apartments for which she was interested in bidding. "Their approval is important to me," she says.

➤ ➤ ➤ ➤ ➤ **Check This List Twice**

Before you finalize on a home purchase or move into a rental, make sure the place is all in one piece. For home buyers, the walk-through usually happens a few days before the close date. For renters, it's less official. Request you see the home one more time before signing any lease papers. This checklist may seem trite, but these little things can add up expensively, and then instead of enjoying your new home, you'll be repairing things that shouldn't be your responsibility as a new resident (and losing money). If any of these procedures fail, don't sign until the management company, the landlord, or the seller fixes it.

- ✓ **Open and close windows:** Confirm they lock properly and don't let in awful drafts.
- ✓ **Turn the lights on and off:** Verify all electrical outlets work.
- ✓ **Run the garbage disposal:** Fixing this later can personally cost you hundreds.
- ✓ **Run the water:** Make sure it's not brown. My building is always doing pipe work, which turns our water brown. Grossness.
- ✓ **Look under every sink for leaks:** Even new homes can have leaky pipes.
- ✓ **Flush toilets:** Does the toilet keep running, like, forever after you flush? Mine does and it kills me!
- ✓ **Test heating and air-conditioning:** I wish I had my heater replaced by the previous owner before I moved in. After one winter with

limited heat, I asked my building manager how much it would cost to replace the thirty-year-old rickety contraption that was built into the wall: $1,900.

➤ ➤ ➤ ➤ A Cure for Closing Costs

They're inevitable and mandatory: all the fees and payouts at the closing date. I think I wrote about six or seven checks at my closing to pay for the appraiser, the title company, the government, my lawyer, etc., etc. Yeesh. Generally, the total amount typically adds up to 3 to 6 percent of the home's purchase price, and while the regulations on them tend to be extremely rigid, there are ways to bring down your closing costs.

Reference your credit. If you have Grade A credit, you can challenge some of the bank's closing costs. Some banks may even let you roll your closing costs into the loan to take away the pressure of paying all that cash up front. You may also earn a lower interest rate on the mortgage if you have a solid credit score.

Wheel and deal. Developers and sellers may be willing to finagle your financing and pay your closing costs to speed up the deal. The buyer doesn't totally escape the closing costs; the fees are attached to the home's sale price, thus increasing mortgage payments. For example, if your closing costs total 5 percent of the home's purchase price, you may be able to ask the seller to increase the purchase price by 5 percent. The seller then uses that money to pay off your closing costs. Sounds shady, but it's totally legal!

Call up your bank. If you're refinancing your mortgage, talk to your original bank. To keep your business, the lender may offer to streamline your mortgage application process, which can end up, at least, saving you application and appraisal expenses.

RENTERS' RELIEF

So I went through all these details and examples of how to buy a home, realizing that most of us rent—but, hey, I gotta try, right? I can't deny that for most of us, renting makes complete sense, especially if we aren't expecting to live in a particular area for too long. It's also difficult to buy if you have no savings for a down payment, no established credit, or no way to lure Mom, Dad, or Aunt Joan into buying property with you. And while rent is money wasted down the drain, there are ways to minimize the loss until you're ready to own.

Smart spending, networking, and negotiating helped Brittany strike a rental deal.

MEET BRITTANY

Age: twenty-four

Hometown: Belle Mead, New Jersey

Schooling: Rutgers University

Dream job: award-winning television news anchor

Favorite adult beverage: a classic vodka club

Most-lusted NKOTB member: Joey McIntyre—"I was die-hard—that hat with the top cut off! Priceless!"

My friend Britt graduated from Rutgers University in 2006 with a journalism degree. A few months later, she landed a sweet TV job in Manhattan, working alongside yours truly at thestreet .com TV. For the first six months, she was living at home with her parents in New Jersey. The decision to stay with the parentals, as she described it, offered free, great food; free laundry; free parking; free cable/Internet/phone; no utilities; and, most awesomely, no rent. But all of that (sorry, Mom and Dad) wasn't enough to keep her from itching to leave and find a place of her own.

Why Move? Her commute was killing her. She spent two hours each way between central New Jersey and Wall Street, costing her a ton of money and her sanity. It was buses, trains, and automobiles for poor Britt four hours a day. She spent a great deal of her income on gas, parking, and train and bus tickets, not to mention that the two-hour commute was keeping her from having much sleep or a social life.

Weighing Her Options. With her starter salary, Brittany calculated there was no feasible way to afford rent in Manhattan, at least not in a location that was safe and relatively near work in the financial district. Her next best location was Hoboken, New Jersey, which is less than a twenty-minute ride on the PATH train to Wall Street. Rent there is about 40 percent less than Manhattan prices. "I sat down with my dad and calculated all of my necessary expenses (rent, car payment, cable, utilities, commuting costs, food, savings contributions, etc.). I also factored in the fact that my commuting costs would be less if I lived closer to the city, and then saw how much was left. Of that amount, we tried to see how much I could afford to spend on rent and still manage to put a little bit away."

Finding a Place. Britt didn't use a broker. Instead she relied on her connection of friends and friends of friends. As it turned out, a friend from high school knew a guy who lived in an apartment in Hoboken that was to be vacated in a couple weeks. The landlord hadn't yet found new tenants. She jumped on it.

Finding Roommates. Brittany discovered that a friend from her hometown was also anxious to break free from her parents' house.

As for the third roommate, Britt invited in on the lease a friend of a friend. "As long as I knew someone who could vouch for the person's sanity, I was fine with it. I really wasn't into the random-roommate thing," she says.

The Dilemma. Much to Britt's shock, the landlord was jacking up the price of the rent, after five years of keeping it steady. She assumed she would get the same rate as the current renters, but at the last minute, she discovered it was not only going to cost her more but that it was no longer affordable.

Her Solution: Negotiate. She called the landlord and told him all the roommates were in love with the apartment, but as young, recent graduates (those were her exact words), they just couldn't afford to pay the new, raised rent. "I proposed a compromise," says Britt, "that we would sign a two-year lease, pay an amount in between the original and the raised rent for the first year, and then pay slightly more the second year."

The Result: Approval. "To my absolute shock—he was completely open to the suggestion, and ended up taking our offer. We signed a two-year lease for the exact amounts I had proposed."

What Convinced the Landlord? With only two weeks until the first of the month and still no tenants, the landlord accepted Britt's offer, rather than paying a broker's fee to find new tenants. Signing with Brittany also meant saving time and energy showing the apartment. Not to mention, the landlord's wife was also a Rutgers graduate. "He may have felt some additional compassion."

RENTERS' INSURANCE: A LESSON IN HOW NOT TO GET SCREWED

Britt doesn't have renters' insurance because she's afraid it's too expensive. But it's really much more affordable than you'd expect, especially when you factor in how much it can save you in the event of a robbery or fire. Think about it: We're quick to insure our lives, our cars, sometimes even our body parts (think JLo and her fabulous ass); but we, too often, neglect to insure the very prized possessions under our roofs with renters' insurance. Imagine you come home to discover your roommate left the door unlocked and suddenly your Nintendo Wii, baseball card collection, and MacBook are all gone and you have no legal recourse. The half-open bottle of Corona is also mysteriously missing.

Who Has No Excuses. If you have stuff you need to protect, then you need renters' insurance. Plain and simple. Your building owner's insurance policy probably won't replace your laptop, sofa, and $200 pair of jeans in the event of a blaze or burglary. A landlord's or management company's policy usually covers damage to the overall building, not the individual apartment units and the property inside. Also, one policy per unit isn't necessarily enough. Experts say roommates should get individual policies.

What It Protects. Renters' insurance generally covers the loss of personal property in cases of theft, storm damage, and fires, but usually not in cases of floods and natural disasters. The insurance also helps in cases where a tenant would be legally liable. For example, if someone slips and falls in your home and decides to later sue you, a renters' insurance policy would likely have you covered.

The Two Types. "Actual cash value coverage" pays the depreciated value of the lost or damaged assets. "Replacement cost coverage" covers the cost to replace an item. The premium on this is usually 10 percent more, according to the Insurance Information Institute.

What It Costs. Renters' insurance costs about as much per month as what you paid to go see the *Rocky Horror Picture Show* at the local theater last Saturday: $12 (that may have included a soda, but def no popcorn). It varies by state, but insurance agents will also want to get an inventory of your property to calculate how much coverage you'll need.

Discount Options. "Multilining," or buying various insurance policies from one source—like renters' insurance and life insurance—can sometimes result in a reduced rate. Some insurers will also offer a discount for having preventive devices like smoke detectors and fire extinguishers.

➤ ➤ ➤ ➤ ➤ **Sublet Safely**

Sublets are a great way to ensure your rent gets paid while you leave for an extended period of time, whether it's to do some traveling or relocate. But then there's the nightmare of coming back to your apartment to face an unhappy landlord who says he won't give back your security deposit because the twenty-one-year-old summer intern who was staying in your studio while you were backpacking through Eastern Europe spilled red wine and somehow, kerosene, on the wall-to-wall white carpet. Also, this idiot somehow managed to punch through your bedroom wall so now there's a hole into your kitchen. Avoid falling victim to a sublet gone bad. Follow these precautions:

Get permission. Make sure you're allowed to sublet your apartment. Ask your landlord.

Get references. Call past landlords for references on prospective subletters. Try to do a credit check, too.

Draft a contract. Write a detailed contract that specifies the length of the sublease, the address, the amount of rent, and when it's due. Include clauses that say the subleasee is financially liable for damages and unpaid rent. You can find some basic templates online by Googling "sublet contract."

Get a deposit. Collect a security deposit to cover any damages. Take photos and make a list of everything in the apartment, and have the subleasee review it and sign it. Change the name on all utility bills for the duration of the sublease to avoid getting slapped with a hefty electric or phone bill.

Get a friend to check in. If you're going to be far and away for an extended period of time, designate a local friend to check in on the apartment once or twice to make sure all's going well and that, indeed, no walls have been damaged and your fridge hasn't been replaced by a keg-orator.

➤ ➤ ➤ ➤ Moving Made Cheaper

Is your time money? Well, so is the case with any mover you hire to help you pack and move your stuff.

Save on supplies. Get boxes for free by asking the local grocery or hardware store to set aside a dozen or so for you at the end of the day. Ask a friend who recently moved if he or she has any spare boxes and extra packing tape lying around. Maybe you can get some from the office, too. Use your old stack of newspapers or magazine pages, instead of buying bubble wrap, to safeguard your fragile items.

Have a packing party. Some moving companies boast packing all your stuff up nicely and neatly, in addition to loading, unloading, and driving the truck. Skip that expense and, instead, pack everything yourself. It may require a whole day's worth of sweat (and back bending), but look at it this way: You will know where everything is once you arrive at your new place and, along the way, you may discover some things are worth trashing. (My friend Matt, who's moved three times since graduating from college in 2005, believes, "If you haven't used it in a year and a half, throw it away.") Invite friends, buy 'em pizza, and make it into a social event.

Buy insurance. If you hire a professional moving company, take them up on their offer for insurance. In case your prized possessions get chipped, cracked, or lost during the move, you'll have some legal recourse.

Haul ass. By no means rule out moving your stuff on your own, although I cannot promise it won't be an absolute nightmare. There's also the risk of getting a hernia from trying to lift your 400-pound dresser yourself. But my editor, Lindsay, lived to tell her story of moving out of her fourth-floor walk-up apartment with no professional help. The payoff: She figures she saved at least $500.

CHAPTER 9

CRUISE CONTROL
A Minicourse in Buying or Leasing a Car

While I've never owned a car, or driven one regularly since
the twelfth grade, I do know from friends and family and this one
classic episode of *Who's the Boss* (the one where Tony buys spoiled
teen daughter Sam that bright yellow clunker of a sedan) that you
can definitely get defeated at the dealership. You can more or less
end up with a car that's (1) a complete piece of crap and/or (2) far
too expensive. For this chapter I've enlisted the advice of car-
buying experts and good friends for the necessary dos and don'ts.
Indeed, this is a whole chapter on cars and all that's related to cars
(including insurance and gas), all *pour vous*. The auto gurus tell
me buying a car is normally the second biggest buy you can make
after a home—hardly chump change. This chapter will help you
be smart about getting your new—or used—wheels.

IS A CAR *WORTH* IT TO YOU?

Notice the question's not, *Can you afford a car?* If your job is a
thirty-minute commute, you don't live near public transportation,
and no one can offer you a ride, you may need to hunker down

and buy a car, just something to get you safely from point A to point B so your boss doesn't fire you for being late or sweaty (from riding your bike to work). A car, in this scenario, *is* worth it to you and you'll just have to find a way to pay for it.

Now, if you're struggling to pay rent on your $700-a-month studio apartment in Chicago and Cookie Crisps are your meal du jour (breakfast *and* dinner), the answer *may* be more like *no*. You could move to a place that's charging $350 a month, better integrate the USDA food pyramid into your daily diet, and find money to spare on a car, but is that worth it to you? It may be if a car is part of your good-life equation, considering (1) the ladies dig it and (2) you can use it to escape on the weekends to your aunt's lake house. Whatever you decide, note this: Experts advise spending no more than 15 percent of your monthly income on car payments (including the purchase price, repairs, oil changes, insurance, gas, and the occasional Turtle Wax). If you can shift your monthly expenditures around by 15 percent to make room for a car *and* it's worth it to you, keep reading.

Case in Point. Remember my friend Dustin who deferred his student loans? He's been living in Los Angeles, where there's something like three cars for every person. But for the past five years he's gotten around without wheels. He travels by public bus, which admittedly cramps his style, but it allows him to read the *L.A. Times* or catch up on sleep during the morning ride and be more prepared for work. He figures having, driving, and maintaining a car would cost him $600 a month, after factoring in his insurance and Cali's outrageously high gas prices. Opting for public transportation allows D to live more comfortably in West Hollywood with one roommate instead of three. He's also using his extra money to pay for a few meals out with friends and an evening film-writing class, as he's an aspiring filmmaker. He also needs that money for tickets to fly back home to PA to visit his family. That's Dustin's good-life picture, and there's just no room for a car, given his desires and monetary situation. Now if he could just find a producer to make his movie!

➤ ➤ ➤ ➤ **Shopping for Auto Insurance**

Once again, you come face to face with your credit score. This three-figure number is the biggest determining factor on setting your insurance cost, among other financial rates. On average, Americans spend close to $900 a year on auto insurance, or $75 a month. These tips will inevitably help you save.

Boost your credit score and improve your credit report, if need be. If there are mistakes on your credit report, fix them before getting a car and buying auto insurance. If you still have some debt to pay off, do so, even if it means waiting another six months to clean up your financial act. The credit poor get don't get rewarded.

Scour the Web. Comparison shop for the best rates at cool sites like www .Esurance.com, www.insure.com, and www.allinsurance.com.

Reward yourself. If you're in grad school and have a B average or better, tell your insurance agent. That may help you save on your premium.

Combine your auto insurance with any other insurance plan you have. For example, if you have existing life insurance or home insurance, see if that agency or insurance provider offers auto insurance, too. You can save when you give extra business to an existing insurance company you work with.

Raise your deductible. Increasing your deductible, or the amount you agree to pay out-of-pocket in the event of an accident repair before the insurance kicks in, can help you save on your monthly premium. Not a bad way to free up your monthly cash flow. Just make sure you have enough money in a piggy bank somewhere to save your butt in the event of an emergency. The rule of thumb is that by raising your deductible $500, you can save up to 30 percent a month on your premium.

Drive a safe car. Luckily most modern cars come with air bags, power-lock breaks, and other safety devices that insurance companies love enough to lower your premium.

Don't drink and drive. Don't hold a baby on your lap while driving, or run red lights, or speed, or do anything that will count against your driving record. A poor driving record means higher insurance.

Nix the Maserati. A fancy car raises eyebrows at the insurance agency— not because it's fancy, but because the agency will lose sleep over the cost to repair the car if it gets wrecked. Lost sleep for the agency means a higher insurance rate for you.

CAN YOU AFFORD TO *PARK* THE CAR?

This may seem like a silly question, but the fact is, parking can be very pricey, especially in big cities. A recent report out of New York City found that people were willing to pay more than $400 a month to park in an underground garage. The most expensive parking spot was going for—get this—$225,000. That, by the way, is also the cost of a two-bedroom condo in New Jersey!

True Story. When my research assistant Tim was in college in Montreal, he decided to park his VW Golf on the street in order to save money. It cost only $60 a year to register his car for curbside parking. Meantime, underground spots nearby would have cost him up to $100 a month. Tim's solution was perfect until winter hit. (Montreal gets an average of 80 inches of snow every winter.) His car spent the majority of each week buried under piles of snow or boxed in by snow-removal trucks parked next to "unused" cars. When Tim needed his car, he had to spend thirty minutes digging it out and then another ten minutes trying to start it up. He eventually caved in and signed up with the underground garage for $100 a month. At least he gave it a try.

DO I LEASE?

A new car becomes a used car the moment you drive it off the lot, instantly depreciating in value. It'll continue to depreciate significantly during the first two years of ownership (up to 40 percent). If money is extremely tight or you need a car for only a short period of time, go for the lease. When you lease a car, you sign for no more than three years after which you can pick another car.

My friend's friend Karla, however, found some drawbacks to leasing. For starters, there are limits to how many miles you can put on your car. Going over that limit means serious fees and charges. So while Karla loved trips to the cottage and road trips upstate, she had to always watch the mileage and make sure she didn't go over. Come to think of it, my dad had this problem, too. He leased an SUV for three years, and the family was all excited, thinking it would serve us well on long car rides, but Dad refused to drive it anywhere except in the neighborhood, worried he'd rack up mileage and concerned it would go through too much wear. After all, leasing a car is essentially borrowing the car from the dealership, and at the end of your term, you have to return it in as close to the same condition as when you got it. That also means you're not allowed to make modifications or additions to the car. Eyeing a new set of rims? Under the terms of most lease agreements, it's not an option.

SHOULD I BUY?

Many assume wrongly that leasing is a better option if you don't have a nice chunk of change in the bank, because they think it's the only way to divide the car payment into monthly installments. The lease ads do a good job of advertising "only $199 a month!" or "pay per month deals!" But when you buy a car, you can pay in monthly installments as well. It may be more expensive when all is said and done, but you do have the option for a more flexible payment plan when you buy a car. We'll get to that later in the chapter.

New or Used?

A used car costs 50 percent less than a new car—hands down. This, of course, means your monthly payments can be significantly lower with a used model. Therein may be your answer. (Bear in mind, the loan on a used car usually has a higher interest rate, but overall, it's a cheaper alternative considering the ticket price, and insurance will be lower. Not to mention, registered used-car owners often pay a smaller motor vehicle excise tax, which is usually calculated factoring in the car's value. In Massachusetts, for example, the excise tax is $25 for every $1,000 of the car's value.)

Also, if you're not particular about options (like a sunroof, satellite radio, and a V6 engine), don't expect to keep the car for too many years (like, no more than four or five), and don't plan on driving much (less than ten thousand miles a year, for example), then you're probably better suited for a used car. The cons of a used car: more maintenance, less warranty coverage than a new car, and, well, it doesn't have that hot-off-the-assembly line new-car smell. Mmmm. But you can always fake it with one of those air fresheners.

Dealership Due Diligence

Come armed and ready for your trip to the auto dealership. Remember our pep talk before braving the cell phone store? Well, this is at least a $20,000 bigger deal. You have a lot of money at stake. Don't forget: You are the boss.

WHAT TO KNOW BEFORE STEPPING FOOT ON A CAR LOT

- ➤ how much the car is being advertised for
- ➤ the original price of the car (also known as the "manufacturer's retail sales price," often found on the car's Web site)
- ➤ what features are included for the price
- ➤ what additional costs need to be factored in (taxes, shipping, etc.)
- ➤ the invoice price (what the dealer spent for the car; once it's out in the showroom, you'll get the sticker price, which reflects the dealer's markup).

P.S. It's unrealistic to buy a new car at the invoice price, but you can use the price for reference to help you during the bargaining process. You can get a copy of the invoice price from many Web sites, like www.edmunds.com, which offers free invoice pricing. Write down what the invoice price is and then ask the dealer what his marked-up price reflects. Make him sweat.

Dealership Dealings

Visit different dealerships and ask for their list price and then the lowest price they can give you. Also ask about any "features" they can throw in, including a CD player, sunroof, free tank of gas, etc. Then thank them and walk out. You're not done yet.

Take the prices and information you got from that first dealership and compare it to a second dealership and a third. When you pit the dealerships against one another, chances are you'll get them to drop their prices. Even though the dealers all sell the same make of cars, don't be fooled; their prices are not the same! Different dealerships have different quotas to fill or different ties to the automaker. So make sure you look around to get the best deal.

Bargaining. I know it's hard to bargain when you're a shy person or when you just want the whole process to be over with. But consider this: Salespeople hate missing out on a sale when they've put considerable time and effort into the process. Seeing someone about to walk out the door after working on the deal all morning can often force the sales rep to meet your terms of sale. Or to call you shortly thereafter.

When you bargain, use your research to seek a better price. If Internet ads show the car sale-priced at $25,000, tell the salesperson you've seen it for around $20,000. Even if the salesperson marks it up to $23,000, you've still received a cheaper quote. It's not lying. It's business.

A "Lot" Saved. Often, cars that are "on the lot" will be cheaper than cars that have to be shipped in from the auto plant (*on the lot* simply means that the car is at the dealership already). If it already has the features you're looking for and it's the color you want, it's a faster, easier, and cheaper way to get your car. If you want to customize your vehicle to suit more specific tastes, you may have to wait a few weeks and pay a little more for the car to be shipped over from the plant.

Mind the Model. Do you *really* need the latest model or will you take one that's slightly older? Next year's Honda Civic will undoubtedly cost more than this year's model if both are available. If it's not a big deal to you, then maybe buying a new car with the older year is a better decision. It's still on the lot and still a brand-new vehicle; it'll just be priced for a quicker sale.

Ask to See the "Demonstrator." This is the car the dealer lets potential customers test-drive. These cars are usually sold when they are a few months old and have several thousand miles on the clock. The advantage: You should save a few thousand dollars off the price.

Cash Is King

If you're paying for the car in cash, you could save money by taking advantage of special discounts and rebates. Tell the dealer upfront that you want to pay in cash. You'll be able to reap significant discounts if you don't require financing. (Note: Dealers like to finance, yes, when the buyer needs a loan. They prefer to be the agent giving you the loan versus you getting a direct bank loan.)

THE BEST TIME TO BUY

Start shopping toward the end of the model year, when dealers are trying to make room for next year's models. This is usually in the fall, but it varies by manufacturer.

The end of the week or the end of the month are also opportunities to snag a good deal. Meeting sales quotas is often more important to the salesman than price when the end of the period comes around.

FINANCING YOUR WHEELZ

Experts advise buying a car that you can afford to pay off in forty-eight months. Try to also have at least 20 percent in cash to put down on the car. (Don't fall for the "no money down" deal; that just usually means a higher monthly interest rate or higher payments. More on that in a sidebar.) To qualify for a car loan you typically need to show:

- ➤ monthly income of $1,600 or more
- ➤ you've lived at the same address for at least six months
- ➤ you're employed and making money (or have a large balance in your bank account)
- ➤ a year of established credit with no black marks
- ➤ a strong credit score

The Dealer Isn't Always the Best Deal. Dealer financing is often more expensive than car loans through banks, credit unions, and independent lenders. Sometimes, an auto dealer may even make more profit from the financing than from the sale of the car. Get quotes from both the dealer and a financial institution.

Credit Check. It always comes down to your credit score, doesn't it? Well, you can bet the rates you're charged on a car loan will be based on it. So, by improving your credit, you may be able to get a better rate on your loan, which may mean you need to take time before you buy a car.

Refinancing. Often, you can wait about six months and then refinance your car loan down to a lower rate. Many lenders pay off your current car loan, and then you pay them back at a new, lower

APR, or annual percentage rate. Sometimes it helps to get a reference letter from your boss telling the lender how wonderful and responsible you are. If you've worked overtime and won some sort of award, have the boss mention that as well. Lenders want to know that they're working with someone who is responsible, knows the meaning of a deadline, and, above all, is dependable. If you're still fresh out of college and had good marks while in school, it doesn't hurt to include a copy of your transcript. Again, it proves that you're a good client to work with.

➤ ➤ ➤ ➤ **0% Auto Financing: What the Heck Is This and Should I Do It?**

U.S. auto manufacturers just looove to boast about 0 percent financing as an incentive for us to buy their cars and boost their otherwise crappy sales records. Typically it means 0 percent interest and zero payments for a certain period of time, like thirty-six months. A few things to note: 0 percent financing is often a shorter term loan than a standard car loan, which means the monthly payments are bigger. Second, to qualify for 0 percent financing, your credit has to be immaculate. And third, the alternative to a 0 percent financing offer is usually a generous rebate. Experts have always argued that it's generally better to pick the rebate over 0 percent financing and, instead, shop around for a low rate from another lender. The math speaks for itself:

Loan	Term	Rebate	APR	Monthly Payment	Total
$15,000	36 months	$0	0 percent	$417	$15,012
$15,000	60 months	$3,000	6.5 percent	$235	$11,100
					Difference: $3,912

➤ ➤ ➤ ➤ ➤ **Don't Get Gas Guzzled—Quick Ways to Save on Gas**

Don't drive. Ha-ha. No, seriously. Can you join in on a carpool or take public transportation? Again, this may be "uncool," but my advice is to make it into an eco-friendly claim. "I'm helping the planet, man. Don't be such a hater." Or, "I'm just doing what Al Gore would do."

Go for the cheap gas. Unless your car has a high-performance engine and your manufacturer recommends a high-octane gas, use the less expensive gas. Premium gas costs 10 to 15 percent higher than regular. And if you're spending $100 a month on gas, that's easily $15 saved.

Warm up in motion. The engine warms up faster when driving than it does when idling, and idling wastes about a quart of gas every fifteen minutes.

Slow and steady. Accelerating too fast wastes gas. Get to full speed slowly. Stop-and-go acceleration consumes more gas, too.

Tire tip. Check your tire pressure regularly. You can lose up to 6 percent in gas mileage for every pound of underinflation.

Invest in maps. Plan your trip and have a current set of maps to help guide you to your destination in good time. In some cases, if you drive far and away a lot and have a tendency to get lost, a solid GPS system could pay off in the long run. This way you avoid wasting gas by driving in circles.

Pack a lunch. You and your friends have planned the ultimate road trip. Don't let high gas prices get in your way. Instead, find ways to save *during* the trip, like packing a lunch instead of eating out at every destination. Also forget souvenirs no one will ever savor. Send postcards instead.

OLIVIA AND HER AUDI

My college friend Olivia dreamt of owning her own Audi since grade school. Her rich next-door neighbor (with perfect clothes and perfect white teeth) always had the newest and latest Audi, and Olivia remembers lusting after a shiny black one of her own for her sixteenth birthday. But she wouldn't actually drive one until her late twenties, when while working as a senior analyst at a pharmaceutical company in New Jersey, she would use her fat year-end bonus to help finance a $45,000 brand-new, black leather interior Audi A4.

Why Didn't She Settle for a Honda? True, the Accords are pretty snazzy these days, and Olivia could have saved $20,000, at least, by opting for a compact nonluxury vehicle. But there's nothing like fulfilling a childhood wish when you're old enough to afford it. That said, this wasn't an entirely emotional purchase for Olivia. She also factored into the purchase that (1) she was single and had the extra cash, (2) her commute to work was a long thirty minutes, and (3) she often made six-hour drives to Pittsburgh to visit her folks. She decided she wanted a car that was extremely reliable and safe. In 2006, the Audi A4 was ranked among the best by J.D. Power and Associates for body and interior quality and overall performance and design.

Paying It Down. Olivia put down 20 percent. The Audi dealership had offered her a 6 percent rate on a loan to finance the rest, but Olivia went with the low 3.7 percent rate from her local credit union. (See? Shopping around pays!) Her monthly payments ended up being around $475. She also purchased the car, instead of leasing it, because, to put it in her words, "I wanted to drive the car into the ground." She wanted a car for the long term, knowing that when she'd finally pay off the loan in four years, she would likely then be ready to have a family with her live-in fiancé / soon-to-be husband. At that point, a lavish car like an Audi would not seem as guilt-free a purchase, considering all the other, bigger expenses, like a home and diapers. "Given my age and where I was in life, I knew that buying this car was going to be the one big purchase of my life that I could splurge on," says Olivia. Her next car, she suspects, will be an Asian car with one of those tough-to-beat five-to-ten-year warranties. And P.S. Experts say you shouldn't finance a car longer than three or four years. If you're stretching out the payments for longer, revise the plan or reject it altogether. Another good rule of thumb is that your car payments shouldn't exceed the life of your warranty.

Surviving the Dealership. Olivia had heard it would be tough bringing down the price of a luxury car. With that in mind, she bought the car at a place that came recommended by her boyfriend's brother, a mechanic who worked closely with the dealership. The referral won her a discount, albeit pretty small. She also thinks having her boyfriend present was helpful. "Bring someone who's experienced, whether it's someone who knows about cars, or a parent," says Olivia.

Looking Back, the One Thing That Made the Deal. Fancy cars typically carry big service costs . . . unless, you have financial protection. Olivia's shiny black Audi came with a maintenance program that covers all oil changes, windshield wiper replacements, and other services for up to fifty thousand miles or four years, whichever comes first. Knowing that many European auto companies are getting rid of their service warranty plans, she doubts she would be able to afford the car today without it.

The 3K Rule

Change the oil and oil filter in your car every three thousand miles. More frequent oil changes will extend the life of your engine and keep your car running cleanly and efficiently. The end.

What She Could Have Done Without. "I could have turned down the extra options—Bose stereo, navigation system, satellite radio, and sports package, which came with sports suspension and nice rims—that's really what kills you." She figures all the add-ons cost her an extra $100 a month.

➤ ➤ ➤ ➤ Let Go of a Lemon

If your car keeps acting up and you find yourself at the mechanic for the same problem time and time again, find out whether your state's "lemon law" can help you out. Typically if your car has a manufacturer's warranty that's yet to expire, and you've had at least three problems in a row over a short time frame, you have the right to get your money back, a replacement vehicle, or some sort of deal. Before you go wasting money on a lemon law attorney to defend your case, make sure you've (1) made a few attempts to *fix* the problem, (2) are sure the defectiveness is something covered under the manufacturer's warranty (check the manual), and (3) you've sent a written letter to the manufacturer stating your situation. Keep all your paperwork from the mechanics.

Keep in mind that various states have different lemon laws with different clauses. Lemonlawamerica.com can help hook you up with a lemon law attorney in your area.

CHAPTER 10

SOCIAL CENTS

Life's a Party. Don't Poop Out for Being Broke.

One of my most successful nights (financially speaking) while getting jiggy in New York was the time I got kicked out of the Marquis nightclub on Ninth Avenue. We paid $25 to get in and $8 per drink and danced for about an hour and a half. But only halfway finished with my adult beverage and two minutes into Michael Jackson's "Billie Jean," my night came to a shrieking halt when a wasted dancer spilled his full glass of vodka tonic down my shirt. No apologies. No sorries. Just "Whoops!" As soon as my friend MJ saw me soaked in booze, he confronted said wasted dancer and demanded an apology. But that only made him more hostile. Push came to shove (literally) and drunken dancer lost his balance and fell on top of a glass table, drinks everywhere. The manager arrived on the scene, demanding to know what happened, and even though MJ and I were completely sober (he doesn't drink and I could afford only one), we were the ones forced to leave. Turns out, drunken dancer was a friend of a friend of a friend of the bar owner. Go figure.

But before we left, MJ and I insisted we get our $25 cover back. It was only midnight and we still had four more potential hours to stay and hopefully sight a celebrity, we argued. (I also mentioned I was a producer for NY1 News, whose viewers would be curious to know which hot night club in Manhattan was kicking out sober patrons over aggressive drunkards with loose connections.) The manager concurred. We felt victorious (and richer). My shirt had already dried up and I would forever have a hot story to tell about how I "got kicked out of a night club."

The lesson: Always get your money's worth, even if you're getting booted out of a dance hall . . . which brings me to this very critical chapter on how to eat, drink, dance, and be merry without going broke. If being social is part of your "good life" equation (and I hope it is), the advice you're about to read can seriously help you save.

My coworker Matt, in fact, just started a Web site that lists all things free in New York City every day, from food to drinks, from theater to karaoke. In the final chapter I'll tell you how he managed to start this superpopular site, www.sageurbanite.com, while working full-time (and by full-time I mean twelve hours a day) as a video producer and editor. But my point with Matt in this chapter is that if you're really determined to pay as little for as much fun as possible, you have options and probably more than you thought. Matt's site proves that even in New York, the most expensive city in the country, there is such a thing as a free lunch, and free music and free art exhibits. . . . No doubt, your town has deals hiding around, too.

PAINTING THE TOWN RED ON LITTLE GREEN

Cabs: Make It a Hybrid Journey

Starting with transport: First and foremost, going out for a drinking good time should always involve a designated driver. But if that's not possible, see what public transportation is available, as it lets you avoid operating heavy machinery, too. In New York, subways are always the cheapest (and often quickest) way to get from point A to point B. But sometimes (especially when I'm lazy) a cab hits the spot. For example, journeying from the Upper West Side to the Lower East Side of Manhattan, where all the fun goes on, is almost like crossing an ocean. There's no convenient way to do it with the subway since it means taking up to three different trains to get to your destination. The bus is out of the question, unless I don't mind getting to the LES two days later. Cabs, in short, are expensive . . . unless you use a *hybrid* form of transportation. And I'm not talking Prius.

When I have to go long distances, say from the Upper West Side to the Lower East Side or even farther to my hipster friends in Brooklyn, I'll sometimes take the subway to the edge of my destination, then hail a cab to take me the rest of the way. I end up saving more than $20 that way. It's even better if you take a cab with a friend or three because you can split the bill.

Once I was getting a ride home in a cab and realized after I got in the car that I wouldn't have enough money for the *whole* distance. I had enough for about three-fourths the drive, so I still took the cab and instead got dropped off ten blocks early. (Dear Mom, I live in a safe, bustling neighborhood where 2 A.M. is not unsafe. People are out all the time. Besides, would it have been safer to stand alone underground for a subway at 2 A.M.?) My other alternative was to stop at an ATM and ask the cab driver to wait. But I walked the rest, happy that I was still able to enjoy a comfortable ride for most of the trip home and save myself the embarrassment of asking the cab driver to stop and let me grab more cash, which I have done once in the past. Okay, four times.

Clubs

Be an Early Bird. Go out dancing in the early part of the week, like Monday or Tuesday, when there are usually low or no cover charges. On the weekends, too, if you get to the club before 9 P.M., there's sometimes no cover. And for clubs that have an attached restaurant, sometimes it's worth grabbing dinner there first. Diners can usually get into the club through an alternate internal entrance, cover free.

Be Aware. If you don't mind your inbox getting inundated, sign up for nightclub promoters' and deejays' e-mail lists to learn about free events. You could save as much as $25 on entrance fees. For better filtering, set up a separate e-mail address for social events and alerts.

Refuse to Pay. If you're not dead set on going to a particular club and have other options, sometimes refusing to pay the cover works in your favor. Or, try saying, "I have no cash," or "I'm short on cash." Depending on how sympathetic the bouncer is (and how many cute girls there are in your group), you may manage to score free cover. See, I told you your good looks could save you money! (Sorry, fellas, but the free-entrance trick usually only works for the ladies.)

Adult Beverages: Champagne on a 7UP Salary

Pregame. We never left our apartment in college on a Friday or Saturday night without having two to six adult beverages (each) before hitting the town. Why? Because it meant we'd spend less at the bars where we could easily pay four times as much for alcohol. (Think about it: A six-pack of Amstel Light costs $10, while a single bottle at the bar runs $5.)

Pay Per Drink. *Never, ever* open a tab at the bar with your credit card! The consequence can easily be one monstrous bill at the end of the night. Instead bring cash and pay for each individual drink at a time. Remember, tipping is about $1 per drink if you pay individually. It's otherwise expected you pay 15 to 20 percent on a tab, which is generally more money, too. Especially do not open a tab if the bartender asks to keep your license along with the credit card. This one time a bartender gave away my license and credit card to the wrong, drunkedy-drunk person. I don't know who was more stupid: me for giving away my very important ID to a bartender, the bartender for not realizing she had mismatched cards, or the drunk guy who was too inebriated to realize he had gone home with a female ID and the wrong credit card.

Make Friends with the Bartender. My friend Kat's friend Davey is the bar owner of a great Irish pub in New York City called Solas. Of all the twenty-five or thirty times I've been there, I think I've paid for a few gin and tonics. Thanks, Davey!

Don't Get Too Generous. Unless your best friend had a bad breakup, got promoted, got engaged, or quit her job, hold off on getting your crew several rounds of shots. That's $25 per round and money you might want later in the week to pay for your daily afternoon grande mocha latte craving from Starbucks.

Get Happy. Don't forget about happy hour (usually between 5 and 8 P.M. on the weekdays) when popular drinks cost half as much. Some bars also put out free food or snacks for the after-work crowd, too. In college, Chili's had Wednesday-night dollar margaritas and all-you-can eat nachos, a delicious and inexpensive dinner meal.

BYOB. Find out what restaurants have a bring-your-own-booze policy and go there. Figure that a solid bottle of red from the liquor store costs $10 (or if you're like me and enjoy the Yellowtail, $6), versus at least $25 for a bottle from the restaurant. That's a guaranteed 50 percent savings on alcohol.

Eating Out

Split the Meal. Entrees are so supersized à la The Cheesecake Factory, they're fit for two hungry stomachs. You can easily save 50 percent by splitting one meal with another friend.

Don't Finish Your Plate. Remember you'll be hungry again tomorrow. If you do get your own meal and the burrito is, indeed, bigger than your head, save some for lunch the next day. Rationalize an expensive meal by promising to spread the cost over the next day's lunch or dinner by eating the leftovers.

Buy the Sunday Paper. The coupon inserts sometimes include discounts for popular chain restaurants. Did somebody say Sizzler?

Show Up Late. My friend Michelle used to always meet her girlfriends toward the tail end of the dinner, just in time to pull up a chair and order coffee or a drink. Her strategy: Cook her dinner at home or pick up a less-expensive slice of pizza. And agree to meet the gang a couple hours later, before the group headed for the bars. She never missed out on too much social fun, since the excitement usually started at the bars and beyond. And she saved herself an average $50 a pop.

Show Up Early. If there's a trendy (read: expensive) restaurant you're desperate to check out, go for brunch versus dinner. The menu is probably less expensive and there may be a prix-fixe option that gives you a three-course meal for less than $20 or $25. Sometimes an adult beverage is included, as well! Meantime, dinner at the same restaurant could easily cost double or triple, if you get a few drinks with your meal.

Don't Get Suckered. There's always that one friend who leaves the dinner table early for an other "commitment," conveniently jetting before the check arrives and dropping a $20 as if he's paid generously. "Oh, keep the change," he says and smiles. It's only when the bill arrives that you realize he was $20 short. Make sure your friends don't stiff you and ask that they remember to include the tip and tax on top of their total before leaving.

Wait for Restaurant Week. Several major cities hold restaurant week or some sort of discounted dining event where fancy-shmancy restaurants offer prix-fixe lunch and dinner courses or cheaper eats. Sometimes you have to make a reservation and often the discounted menus during these events are limited to just certain foods, but the savings can be significant. Here are some of the major cities with periodic dining deals throughout the year and where to get more info.

Baltimore, baltimorerestaurantweek.com

Denver, denver.org/denverrestaurant

Hudson Valley, NY, hudsonvalleyrestaurantweek.com

Indianapolis, indyrestaurantweek.com

Long Island, longislandrestaurantweek.com

New York, nycvisit.com/restuarantweek

Philadelphia, centercityphila.org/restaurantweek

San Diego, sandiegorestaurantweek.com

San Francisco, onlyinsanfrancisco.com

Washington, D.C., washington.org/restaurantwk

SAVING ON REC SPENDING

Volunteer. You can get into many museums or events for free by working or volunteering, say at a film festival or a smaller theater company. Spending your time can save your cash. In New York, for example, several off-Broadway theaters like the Astor Place Theatre and Second Stage Theatre use volunteer ushers who get free admission to performances. Boost Mobile Rock Corps offers a free concert ticket in return for community service (visit www.boostmobilerockcorps.org). And the Tribeca Film Festival (www.tribecafilmfestival.org) rewards volunteers with free tickets to screenings. Volunteers are required to make a minimum commitment of three six-hour shifts, doing everything from ushering to stage setup to making Starbucks runs in exchange for admission.

Web Savings. www.stubhub.com: Great for sports, concert, and theater tickets. It's owned by eBay, but the listings are not necessarily identical to what's on eBay. (Note: All sales are final at Stubhub, so if the event gets canceled, you're most likely out of luck.)

www.eBay.com: At last check the auction site had close to sixty thousand listings under "Event Tickets." Use your eBay buying tricks and score a pair of Cirque du Soleil tickets for less.

Craigslist.org: Great for local events. In my experience, sellers on Craigslist are usually in a last-minute bind and can't afford to wait for an auction to end on eBay. In other words, you can sometimes get a steal on tickets. The site also lists cultural events going on in and around your town or city.

www.ticketliquidator.com: The site boasts having some of the lowest prices on event tickets, from Jimmy Buffet to NASCAR, the Yankees, and Vegas shows. The site's database of tickets stem from both brokers and individual sellers. Cool factor: If the event you paid for gets canceled, you can get a refund, something that's not necessarily guaranteed if you buy from Craigslist or Stubhub.

➤ ➤ ➤ ➤ ➤ **Aaliyah's Social Cents**

Who's Aaliyah? I've already mentioned her awesome clothes in chapter 4. She's a friend of a friend, twenty-five years old, from Harlem, loves hip-hop and cafes, and is a self-proclaimed Francophile. She hasn't quite found her "true calling" yet, she tells me, and so she's been doing odd jobs to pay the rent. During the day, she interns at a magazine to gain experience in publishing. By night, she serves tables at a neighborhood bistro. On the side, she's helping a young fashion designer build and design her Web site. Multitasking. It's the New York way. How else do you make rent?

When Aaliyah goes out. Aaliyah enjoys concerts in the city, but with ticket prices costing some serious Ben Franklins, it can be financially daunting. The solution? Aaliyah goes to ticket agents the night of the concert, places such as local record shops and stores that sell tickets outside of the box office and Ticketmaster. Usually the agents are assigned a fixed number of tickets to sell. If they have tickets left over, they can usually make you a deal. "I'll ask them for a two-for-one or ask them to waive the taxes and processing fees," she says. "The concert's in a few hours so they want to get rid of the tickets before they can't get anything for them." That said, Aaliyah has better luck striking deals with these agents for more obscure shows than, say, Kanye West.

➤ ➤ ➤ ➤ ➤ **Bookworm Savings**

Some of my best ideas for this book struck me while typing away at the midtown library in Manhattan. There my free membership card earned me one of dozens of comfy seats near electric outlets where I could plug in my MacBook and hook up to free WiFi. It was my office-away-from-home office (which at the time was just a bar stool along my kitchen counter—not so great on the back). The library was not only worker-friendly, it saved going to Starbucks where I would need to hook up to T Mobile's WiFi ($6 an hour) and keep consuming expensive and burnt-tasting coffee. And I'm apparently not alone. Young adults are heading to the public library more and more these days, as we catch on to their free internet, electronic databases, and quiet chambers. According to researchers at Pew Internet & American Life Project and the University of Illinois at Urbana-Champaign, 21 percent of eighteen-to thirty-year-olds are going to the library versus 12 percent of the general adult public.

Now I know libraries aren't so "cool." Until I started working on my book, I hadn't been in one since my friends and I pulled an all-nighter at Columbia's library for a group writing assignment. We never checked out any books; we just liked the space for its free WiFi and cute business school guys (my project-mate Rachel was on the prowl for a tall, Jewish MBA husband).

Where was I? Oh yeah—the fabulous bibliotheque might be a little bit on the dorkier side, but it's really one big coupon in disguise. Going there can save you on books (duh) but also DVDs. You may be surprised how up to date your local library's collection of films is. It's not just *Mary Poppins* and *Kindergarten Cop*. At last check (as in August 2007), my library up the block was carrying Will Ferrell's *Blades of Glory* and the action-packed *300*—both new releases. And did I mention *free* Internet at the library? You could hope that some neighbor next door or upstairs has an unlocked WiFi account that you can steal, but I've never had much luck with that.

BON VOYAGE. BON SPENDING.

A former coworker once surprised his girlfriend with tickets to the Bahamas. He bought the tickets through Spirit Airlines advertised as $9 each way. After taxes and fees they came to a little more than $100 each, but that, still, was a bargain. He struck the deal after being on an e-mail alert list from Spirit, which gave limited customers a small window frame to hop online the day after Christmas and buy these über-cheap tickets to the Caribbean. Here are some other ways to save for your next big trip.

Fly Off-Peak. If you're looking to strike a deal, the summer months are not your best bet. Travel aficionados tell me the best time to travel is during the fall season, from September to Thanksgiving. The bargains can be hundreds cheaper. Also, avoid booking your trip more than 150 days in advance, since most airlines don't offer discounts or sales until later.

Comparison Shop on the Web. Aggregate searches on the Internet at sites including www.kayak.com, www.sidestep.com, and www.mobissimo.com can give you comprehensive price comparisons on multiple airlines and hotels. The sites www.orbitz.com, www.expedia.com, travel.priceline.com, and travelocity.com are also worth checking out. Keep a pen and paper by your computer to track all the various deals.

Contact the Airline Directly. Sometimes airlines offer exclusive deals only available through their Web site or by calling their travel hotline. Never ignore the airline's own site because the cheapest deals on aggregate search sites can still be a few dollars cheaper when bought directly from the airline. Case in point: To visit mom and dad in their new home in San Francisco, I've often flown Jet Blue and it usually rounds out to be $500 per flight—the cheapest found on aggregate search sites for non-stop itineraries. Then one day I landed on www.virginamerica.com. I'd never heard of it, frankly, since I never recalled seeing the carrier show up on, say, Orbitz or SideStep. I think I just found an ad for it on Google. But get this—the same flight (more or less) totals around $350—a 30 percent discount! Also, if you book a flight and you see it for less later, call the airline and explain the situation. Sometimes they'll refund you the difference.

Travel Agents Are Still Making Money. Sounds shocking, considering I haven't seen a travel agent since I booked my flight to Paris in college for my study abroad program, but travel agents are particularly great in ethnic neighborhoods, where residents travel often to a particular destination. North from where I live there is a huge Dominican population, and there, travel agents often get preferred rates for clients traveling to the Dominican Republic.

➤ ➤ ➤ ➤ **In Case You Break Your Leg in Paris . . . a Tutorial on Travel Insurance**

I know it's so rare that we would get drunk in a foreign country and injure ourselves, but sometimes travel insurance is totally worth it. It can come to the rescue for a medical emergency, in case you lose your luggage, or need to cancel a flight. Here's the skinny.

No-refund trips. If you've planned an expensive prepaid vacation that has a no-refund policy, you may want to consider buying travel insurance in case of an emergency or unforeseen situation. For example, if you've spent $4,000 on a luxury cruise to Greece, you might not get the money back if the cruise line goes bankrupt. In some other cases, travel insurance may cover any hefty fees associated with trip cancellations. Do the math. If you can definitely cancel your tickets and plane reservations with few charges, then consider skipping on travel insurance.

Climbing Mount Everest? Travel insurance can also help if you're taking an active trip where you may get physically hurt, like a hiking, rafting, or skiing adventure. It's particularly important if you're venturing to a foreign land or a remote destination where you have limited access to medical help. In those instances, make sure the insurance covers emergency medical evacuation in order to pay for transportation to the nearest hospital. Otherwise, in the event of a serious injury without travel insurance, you could easily face a bill in the thousands.

Check your existing insurance. Sometimes your health insurance plan already covers your medical treatment overseas. If you have your home owner's policy, it may cover stolen baggage. Just keep in mind that making a claim on your home owner's insurance plan could raise your premium for that plan.

Check your credit-card policy. Some credit-card companies offer travel protection. Call the number on the card's back and find out what assistance is provided. Don't make any assumptions.

Read the fine print. Travel insurance is not always all-inclusive. Many plans exclude financial help in the event of war, preexisting medical conditions, or bankruptcy of certain travel providers. Make sure you're covered for what you need. Travel agents and insurance providers can offer more help.

➤ ➤ ➤ ➤ ➤ Renting a Car on the Cheap

Want to rent a car to drive to the beach? Making an IKEA run and need wheels? Planning a miniexcursion? I was so desperate once to avoid the city's clothing tax, I rented a car to go tax-free shopping in New Jersey for a Saturday. Not so smart. I spent so much on renting the car, I didn't have any money left to spend at the Short Hills Mall.

When you need a vehicle for a short time, either in your own area or when you're away, try these rental savings tips.

Go compact and dial up. Figure out the tiniest-size car you need for the trip, then call around for quotes from various chain and local rental agencies.

Question what's "free." Occasionally, the car-rental company will offer you a "free" upgrade, like to an SUV or an eight-cylinder car, which may seem like a deal, but then again, think about how much *more* you'll have to pay to fill up the car. If the rental agency offers you no other choice but a gas-guzzling chunk of metal, ask for a discount or a free tank of gas to compensate for the higher costs.

Get the itemized total. While you think you've banked on a fantastic base rate for the Honda Civic at the rental agency, your total price could hit the moon once all the taxes and fees are thrown in. Always get an itemized list of all charges, including local taxes, drop-off charges if you're bringing the car back to a different office, as well as any mileage charges and optional insurance. And phone your insurance company or credit-card issuer to see if you can avoid buying the insurance for the rental car.

Jump on deals and discounts. Find out if there are any specials or if you can use your frequent flier miles. Ask about AAA, student, union, or any other discounts. Also, if you find a deal one place but would rather use a different rental company, call and ask your preferred agency if it will match the best-received offer. Sometimes Googling coupon codes or re-serving the car online can help you save, too.

Know the rules. Understand ahead of time how a car-rental agency counts days, since some rental firms will charge you for a whole extra day if you bring the vehicle back just a couple of hours late. Ask about restrictions, too. For example, some rental contracts prohibit crossing a state line or driving on dirt roads.

Consider clubbing. That depends on how often you rent. Club member perks often include no long lines at the counter, quicker service, and frequent driver miles or points toward future rentals. Members also may get discounts on rentals and upgrades. Some car-rental companies charge a membership fee, so make sure it's worth it for you to join. The Web site www.zipcar.com is a popular members-only car-rental agency for busy drivers.

CHAPTER 11

BECAUSE LIFE HAPPENS
Expect and Pay Wisely for the Unexpected

Aside from rent, bills, loans, the car, food, and the occasional adult beverage, we young professionals need money to handle life's inevitable (and blessed) events, namely, falling in love, births, weddings, christenings, and little nephews' Bar Mitzvahs. It's fun to splurge on loved ones, but when you're twenty-five years old making $50,000 (if you're lucky) and find yourself contemplating purchasing a $250 delivery blanket for a friend's newborn, you've appropriately landed in Looneyville. It often requires a sane-minded friend (or in my case, my mom) to talk you out of buying said delivery blanket. For the benefit of future and unexpected purchases for loved ones and friends, best to avoid Looneyville and learn this chapter.

WOOING

Dating can be, among other things, a pain in the stinking wallet. I might be better off if I made my steady pay for everything and, indeed, that strategy works for a lot of people I know, but personally, I just don't believe that's fair on many, many levels, especially because I'm earning a salary that leaves me with some disposable income and I can contribute. (Also, he'd probably dump me for stiffing him all the time.) My friend Christine, who's now married, also didn't believe in letting her higher-salary-earning beau pay *all* the time, or even *most* of the time. "I just don't think it's right," she would say. "We're both in our twenties and trying to save (and eventually buy a house together). I can't expect him to spend all his money on dating me." Nor should you spend all your money dating your significant other should the situation be reversed.

➤ ➤ ➤ ➤ ➤ **Don't Be Sorry You Signed . . .**

An old coworker of mine, Lenny, is happily married with a bouncing baby girl. But his rocky two-year relationship with a lady named Evelyn, which ended a few years before he met his current wife, still haunts him. Evelyn isn't exactly cooking up rabbit stew for Lenny, but a bad breakup left her feeling slightly vindictive. She decided to take her rage out on Lenny's credit by refusing to pay her $89 Limited store-credit-card balance. Now you wonder: How is it that Lenny is getting burned by her relatively small financial mishandlings? Well, the two had cosigned on the card, assuming Lenny would cover Evelyn's bills in the event that she couldn't (or, in this case, outright *wouldn't*). His credit score would be near perfect, he told me, if not for that misstep at the mall in 1999, and now that he is renovating his house and asking banks for lines of credit, his credit history will be under close scrutiny.

In general, you *never* want to cosign on anyone's credit-card or loan application. It's hard enough covering your own financial butt. Why be responsible for another person, especially if this person could end up wanting revenge or just being irresponsible in the future?

Although my steady and I share the cost of everything from Mexican food to the movies to cabs and dark chocolate–peanut

M&M's, we recently discovered we were both being careless with our cash on the weekends. Steady, who lives in Philly, occasionally takes Amtrak to New York to visit and that can add up quickly. Transportation is sort of a cost of dating, since we are technically a "distant" couple, so that's not something we can bin. We both signed up for Amtrak's Guest Rewards, which lets us rack up points toward a free trip or hotel discounts. We also try to make visits less expensive by sometimes replacing our usual $20 (per person) prix-fixe breakfast on Saturdays and Sundays with bagels and coffee. It's sometimes annoying anyway to wait forty-five minutes for a table when we both could be spending the morning walking around the city or just snoozing. We were also taking cabs. Everywhere. (That's shamefully my fault, since I'm kind of lazy and I rationalized the cost of cabs by saying it would always save us time. And time equals money, right?) But sometimes cabs don't save time and they definitely don't save money; $18 versus $4 to get to Greenwich Village from the Upper West Side (one way). It's not hard math.

My point: It's the little things that add up in relationships. And habits/expectations are established from the get-go, so it's best to be honest about your financial situation ASAP. No need to disclose salaries or trust fund statuses by month five. Heck, my steady and I didn't learn each other's salaries until well into our wooship. But thanks to some simple expletives—like "Wow. That's so expensive!"—and a gentle reminder that "It's your turn to pay, isn't it?" and maybe a pseudodramatic "Man, I've got a *stack* of bills to pay this week," we managed to send off the right messages/signals about our paying standards (at least in the short term). I also know that my steady is ambitious and financially responsible. About eight months in we disclosed what, if any, debt we were paying off. He has none, he tells me, except his mortgage. He also pays off his credit card every month. And that, I can say, is pretty exceptional for a twenty-nine-year-old single gent these days. In short, I think we're financially compatible. He doesn't understand $300 shoes, but he does have a $350 smartphone and a car that requires gas. I take the subway in my expensive shoes. I think we balance out.

Random Musing. My friend Kate was dating a man the summer before she began graduate school at Columbia. Before their summer lovin' ended, he wanted Kate to take a cross-country road trip with him that would require renting a Winnebago. She bluntly said she'd love to go but had no money to spend on such adventures, as she was saving up for New York City. However, she *could* offer him company and meals as the roadie chef if he was interested. After all, she had always wanted to see the world's biggest ball of twine. They had a deal. I suppose what I'm random musing about here is that there's totally nothing wrong with being treated on a date or a cross-country excursion here and there. Now, on the other hand, if your steady is an oil tycoon or a Greek shipping heir or carries the last name Hilton or Trump, forget the above. Order the surf and turf and leave your wallet at home.

BEFORE "THE QUESTION"

Way, way, way before modern times (and by *modern* I mean "post-TiVo"), marriage was viewed as a financial contract between the man's and the woman's fathers. And while (most) women (in America) have the freedom to fall in love and independently choose a life partner these days, money still plays an enormous role during marriage. And it is no secret that disputes over money are a top reason why many marriages fail.

Disclosing and discussing financial skeletons in the closet and financial goals should be a must-do before tying the knot. Of course, that's easier said than done; asking each other about money can be like pulling teeth. So to ease matters a bit, and before slipping on the ole promise ring, consider playing with the following questions to get to the real heart of each money matter.

"Ever Get Hounded by a Collection Agency?" This can open doors to discovering each person's financial background. At least six months before the wedding date, couples should have a serious chat about their financial histories and current bank balances. Just lay it all out because it's going to surface sooner or later.

"College Was So Expensive, Right?" This may help unveil debt levels. Along those lines, engaged couples should try to improve their credit score as much as possible before the wedding. This can help tremendously when applying for future loans, like a mortgage.

"Where Do You See Yourself in Ten Years?" This unleashes your steady's financial prospects. Does one of you want to go back to school? Become a volunteer firefighter? Play PowerBall every week and win the lottery? Open a small business? Engaged couples should review their future goals to gain a sense of how much money they may need to save/invest during marriage. Questions should include: How many children do we want? Do we want to send them to public or private school? Do we want to live in the city or the suburbs? Do we want a vacation home? Will your midlife crisis involve buying a Porsche?

➤ ➤ ➤ ➤ **The Prenup Low-Down**

If you think prenuptial agreements are trendy with just the über-wealthy, think again. Especially in a city where couples tend to get married later in life, when each has probably accumulated some type of high-worth asset—be it an apartment, a car, or an inheritance—a prenup could come in handy in the event of a divorce. *Still not convinced?* Consider at least going through the motions of preparing one, experts say. "A prenup gets couples to get it out on the table and talk about the emotional issues related to money, their objectives and goals," says Arlene Dubin, author of *Prenups for Lovers.* "It leads to a conversation that is helpful later in marriage."

WEDDINGS, SHMEDDINGS—*VOW TO SPEND SMART ON YOUR WEDDING*

I get it—it's the biggest day of your life. It has to be special, and if it doesn't meet your expectations, all you will think about during your honeymoon in Fiji (while being served champagne and strawberries on your private beach) is how the caterers cut and served the wedding cake *before* you had a chance to take photos in front of the triple-decker, smashing a big, fat slice into your beloved's face. (Seriously, this happened to a friend of mine and she still brings it up during her weekly therapy sessions.) Not to forget—if your wedding day is a disaster, your marriage will be cursed, like, forever.

But as my clever (and single) friends point out, people are supposed to get married, not *weddinged*, right? So what's with the $20,000 cover band and the $100-a-pop wedding favors?? Now, I'm not pooh-poohing *Great Gatsby* weddings. If you (or your parents, as it may be) have the appropriate funds to splurge on a big, fat wedding, go for it! I would be happy to attend. But if it's going to be a super spending stretch and you have to take on several new credit cards to afford the Bentley limousine or that month's salary of a wedding cake, please, for the longevity of your marriage (since financial trouble is a big cause for divorce), consider these cost savers.

First Things First

Seek references. Surely you have a friend, a cousin, or a coworker who's in the midst of planning a wedding or who recently wed? Neglecting your circle of engaged or newlywed couples is potentially money down the drain. After all, it's always best to learn from others' financial regrets rather than your own. My friend Marissa, whom I met while studying abroad in Paris in college, got married at twenty-seven. Before she started to plan she created an Excel spreadsheet listing all the local newlyweds whom she knew (or whom her mom knew) and their advice. "I asked them what vendors they used for what I called 'The Essential 9': Location, Photographer, Videographer, Florist, DJ/Band, Transportation, Stationary, Cake, Wedding Attire." Her references offered tips off the bat. "I was able to recognize common themes in vendors where they had issues."

Timing

My friend Olivia (the Audi driver you met earlier, in my car chapter) is getting married in December, which will help her save substantially on decorations. The country club where she's having her reception will have big, lit-up Christmas trees in the cocktail lounge and ballroom. There will be wreaths on doors and classic mini white lights throughout. Her church is also going to be neatly decorated for the holiday season, which helps Olivia save on flowers for the ceremony.

Location

If a country club or hotel reception hall costs more than you want to spend, what about a relative's big backyard? Or how about your third cousin's house up in the Poconos? My freshman year roommate,

Bethany, who got married in her hometown of State College, Pennsylvania, suggests some other alternative (and less-expensive) sites, like the local Knights of Columbus hall. State and local parks or restored historic sites may also be worth checking out. Note that some public spaces may have restrictions on alcohol.

Save-the-Dates and Invitations

Several of my friends made their own invitations by visiting a Michaels store and hitting up the Martha Stewart Crafts aisle. My childhood friend Targol, one of the savviest businesswomen I know, adds that the days of hand lettering or engraving invitations are over. She's currently engaged and planning her wedding, and she's come across a lot of cheaper alternatives, like thermography, which is raised lettering that appears as if it's engraved but it's not. "If you have a high-tech printer at home, you can do it yourself," she says. Or visit a local print shop for help. Here are some sites that offer reasonably priced card design and printing services.

> **www.vistaprint.com:** My friend Marissa used this site for printing her save-the-date cards. They often have sales and specials. "Just watch out," she says. "Some of the items may get printed with a small 'vistaprint' logo on the back." It's not that obnoxious, she says, but something to watch out for.
>
> **www.mygatsby.com:** Targol is a big fan of this invitation site for its selection and competitive pricing. The caveat: You have to assemble the invitations yourself. But otherwise, "They're beautifully printed," she promises.

Music

The staff at the reception hall can sometimes refer bands that have played there. But be mindful that there may be a conflict of interest at play. "Most locations have financial deals with bands that they recommend," says Josh Brooks, an event planner in New York City. For less-biased advice, ask married friends and family for their recommendations. The longer you wait to book, the harder and more expensive booking a band may become. If your wedding is on a Saturday night during the busy summer season, reserve a band six months before the big day, if not sooner, says Brooks. Remember, bands usually charge by the member, so the bigger the band, the bigger the cost. A deejay, meantime, can easily save you 50 percent. Note from Marissa: Most bands and deejays do not let you attend a live wedding to hear what they really sound like. But sometimes they offer sessions where you can listen to samplings of what they can play and how they sound. Make sure you go!

Party Favors

This ought to go in my "Just Say No!" chapter. The brides I spoke to unanimously agreed that party favors are a waste of money. Few guests will remember, let alone keep the party favors as souvenirs. But I do remember inhaling Hershey's kisses and candy corn at Bethany's wedding (sweets that really came in handy after the third gin and tonic). She put out seasonal candy on the tables, instead of party favors. "Jelly bellys or M&M's in your wedding colors are fun and pretty cheap, too," says Bethany.

You may also want to consider doing something charitable. Bethany suggested donating to your local charity and placing a nice note next to each place setting that says simply, "The couple has donated to ABC Charity on your behalf." She adds, "Whether you donate five hundred dollars or fifty dollars, no one has to know, and it still counts for something good!"

The site www.receptionfavors.com has some party-favor options for as low as $2 to $3 each with free shipping.

Food

Many venues will charge you an additional cost per head if you want to let your guests choose from a variety of entrees. "Your best bet is to order one meal for everyone, but make it a crowd-pleaser, like a chicken dish or the surf and turf," says Targol (who, incidentally, is getting married on July 4 in Newport, Rhode Island. Since her venue cost an arm and a leg, she found ways to cut costs in other ways). If you have some vegetarians attending, you may want to have a few vegetarian entrees on hand, or offer enough meatless appetizers they can get full on. And, instead of a full dessert bar, opt for a small accompaniment with your cake, like chocolate-covered strawberries, suggests Targol. Here are some other food alternatives:

Finger Food. You can always do hors d'oeuvres instead of a full meal. This works particularly well for odd-time wedding ceremonies, like late night or midafternoon.

Buffets. They tend to be cheaper than served meals. It also saves money spent on gratuities for the cost of the meal for each person.

Go Local. See if local restaurants can cater. Oftentimes you can get your favorite food and set up a buffet yourself.

Photography and Videography

This is not something you want to book off of Craigslist. Many couples would agree it's worth going the extra mile to pay for a recommended photographer and videographer. Marissa offers a good point: If your photographer invests a great deal in advertisements on wedding Web sites, be wary. A popular wedding photographer/videographer books mainly through word-of-mouth referrals. Marissa also suggested finding a photographer who operates on a "half day" rather than "full day" coverage. Always ask to view their previous work. And while he or she may be hard to find, a photographer who doesn't charge by the hour can save you the most money. (Note: A good photographer should also include the negatives and a videographer should supply the raw footage.)

Finally, if hiring a professional film and videographer will totally break your bank, consider hiring a friend or a college student instead. In fact, designate at least one guest to help take pictures—even if they're just candid ones. Better safe than sorry.

Dresses

Ann Taylor and J.Crew carry a small collection of modestly priced wedding dresses, as does Target with its exclusive Isaac Mizrahi bridal gown collection. Bridesmaids dresses in ivory or cream can also help save major bucks on dye. You can add a colored sash to each bridesmaid dress to differentiate it from the bridal gown. Of course, there's also the Filene's Basement annual bridal gown sale (twice a year in Boston) where brides-to-be have been known to walk out with a gown that originally cost $9,000 for less than $700. Check out www.filenesbasement.com/bridal for dates in your area.

CELEBRATING LIFE'S MILESTONES . . . ON THE CHEAP

Just because our friends and family decide to throw a wedding fit for a king and queen doesn't mean *we* should go broke attending. Not to forget the engagement party, the shower (which is not the same as the engagement party, I was informed), and the bachelor/bachelorette bashes. And then later when these couples want to have children, that means baby showers, christenings, Bar and Bat Mitzvahs, Super Sweet Sixteens, and graduations. It never ends.

P.S. Just because I urge spending smartly on gifts for friends and family lovebirds, that doesn't mean we should come off looking like cheapskates. We are classy people. For some help on what gifts to buy when and how much is enough, here's a summary I've put together.

Weddings. Expect to spend $50 to $150, depending on how close you are to the bride/groom. If you bring a date, consider buying a bigger gift from both of you.

Overall, pooling money together with friends/relatives for any big invitation event is a smart way to spend. For example, instead of buying a $100 tea set off the wedding registry on your own, you and a friend might consider pitching in $75 each to buy the tea set and a year's supply of the couple's favorite tea brand. It's a thoughtful, added bonus for the couple who likely won't even realize you spent less as a pair than separately. And if the couple *is* keeping score of who paid how much, they're lame. Don't let them manage your wallet.

Baby Showers/Births. If you attended the baby shower and bought a gift, no need to splurge on another present when the baby is born. Just make sure you go visit the newborn in the hospital or once the little one arrives home. Some flowers for mom would be thoughtful. The range of how much to spend for a newly added member to a family is wide. It's anywhere from $10 to $150, depending on *who's* expecting. If it's a coworker you hardly know, a $10 teddy bear, some baby onesies, or a $25 gift certificate to Baby Gap is plenty. The expecting parents would never have expected you to buy something, so anything you give is beyond thoughtful and considerate. Even then, if you feel like you can't afford a $25 gift card to Babies 'R' Us, or wherever, just don't do it. A simple card of congratulations sent to the couple's home address is also classy. Now, if this coworker is your boss and you have a close working relationship (or you want to kiss up), make a bigger investment, say $35 to $50. Yes, that's right—investment. It pays to please your boss.

Meantime, if it's your sister-in-law who's expecting, go for one of the more *expensive* items on her registry or, say, a $100 gift card to Buy Buy Baby or the like. Save being ostracized from the family. You may even consider organizing the shower at your home or hers. Family should come first.

Christenings. A $50 check (considering our age group) is generally appropriate, etiquette experts tell me. But if this is your godchild, you may want to spend more. A christening also provides a good opportunity to give an alternative to money, like shares of a company or a savings bond.

Bar or Bat Mitzvahs. Think of this as if you're going to a fancy dinner party. How much would you probably spend on good food and a live band? That sometimes helps me rationalize the price of a gift. One Jewish tradition is to give in multiples of $18, the numeric equivalent of *chai*, the Hebrew word for "life." Or if you prefer giving a round number, $100 (again, mindful of our age group) is pa-lenty.

CHAPTER 12

GETTING COVERED
Ways to Beat Our Ill-Forsaken Health-Care System

A few months back I was gathering anecdotes for my book (i.e., eavesdropping on a conversation between a twenty-something woman—let's call her Diane—and her dad over an early dinner in the East Village). Diane had recently chipped a back tooth, she nonchalantly told him over their Caeser salads. She would take care of it "at some point," she promised, but had zero health insurance, so it would simply have to wait, especially since it would cost her in the hundreds to pay for it out of pocket. Dad stopped chewing, bewildered by the comments. "It used to cost five bucks to get a tooth pulled back when I was in college," he reminisced. Now, I am not sure if that was the norm back in the 1960s or if Dad used to visit an unlicensed dentist in some dark alleyway, but my takeaway from their conversation was that older generations have *no* idea the struggles we young adults go through to get and afford basic, basic health care.

After my eavesdropping incident, I was giving a talk at a Blue Cross Blue Shield conference, in 2007, and a reoccurring question at the event was "How can parents better prepare their children for the mysteries of health care once they're on their own?" The truth is, we could all, young and old, use some more education on health insurance. (We could all use some extra money to pay for it, too.) The lack of knowledge not only threatens our livelihoods; it can have severe *financial* ramifications for us down the road. For those reasons, this is perhaps the most important chapter in this book.

And yet many of us bail on health insurance at this stage in our lives because (1) we feel that our vital youth will let us bounce back fast without seeing a doc, (2) we are confident a dose of Airborne with echinacea will do the trick, and (3) we trust that we can pay for our eight cavities when we get a "real job." Wrong, wrong, and wrong.

That's twisted logic. All it really means is that we've let the system defeat us. But that's bogus. We work too hard; we owe it to ourselves and our wallets to take proper and cost-efficient care of our health. Those eight cavities will become root canals before you know it, and a flu gone untreated can snowball tragically into pneumonia. Then you'll really get slapped with a bill from hell.

Paying for health care is a challenge, to say the least, for a majority of Americans, and it is particularly difficult for those of us just starting out in the real world. For years (if we were lucky), our parents' health plans covered our prescription cough syrup, eye exams, and teeth cleanings. When we were in college, our school's health plan also cut us a break for many of our health expenses. Then, before we knew it, many of us got thrown into the nine-to-five world of cubicles, power lunches, and PowerPoint presentations, where we were first introduced to alien forms with titles such as LTD, FSA, PPO, and, my personal favorite, COBRA, a term that pops up when you're in between jobs. Again, this is only if we are *lucky*. Employees are expected to pay out of pocket more and more each year. So even if you're working full-time at a company, health care can still amount to a big expense. And like Diane, you may not even have any employee-sponsored insurance because you're either working part-time or freelance or are in between jobs. But that's no excuse, either. There are ways to get covered. Your health depends on it and, thus, your good life, too.

MY COMPANY DOESN'T PROVIDE HEALTH INSURANCE! (GULP)

Let's start with the most health-care challenged of all of us: those who cannot get group health insurance through an employer. Some of us are self-employed and others may not have full-time gigs with guaranteed discounted group health benefits. But I can bet we'll probably at some point between now and the next ten years get the flu, contract pink eye, or chip a tooth, hopefully not all at the same time. So it's worth it to have *some* basic coverage. (If it makes you feel any better, those of us who *have* discounted group health coverage are still forced to pay more and more out of pocket every year.)

So how to independently buy insurance and avoid paying a fortune? Generally, the cheapest route is getting coverage through your state's HMO, or health maintenance organization. An HMO costs less than buying coverage directly from a health insurance company as an individual, but there are limitations to HMOs. For example, you have to go with a general-practice doctor tied to the HMO plan. Here are some tips to keep in mind before signing up.

Contact Your State Insurance Commissioner's Office. Find out what health programs are offered in your state. Healthy New York, for example, is a state-subsidized program for the self-employed that offers a bare-bones policy at a much lower premium.

Comparison Shop. In some states, like New York, New Jersey, and Maine, everyone has access to health insurance, but that doesn't mean it comes cheaply. You should still shop around. Sites like www.ehealthinsurance.com and www.digitalinsurance.com offer comprehensive quotes from various plan providers.

Create Your Own Group. If you can't get group insurance through your employer, make your own group within the company to earn the reduced rate, which can lower your health-care costs by up to 50 percent. In some states, a "group" constitutes as two or more employees who work at least twenty-five hours per week.

Join the Freelancers Union. Or some other nearby association, like the local chamber of commerce, that may offer a group health plan, again, with the discounted premiums.

Decide on the Extras. Once you've settled on an HMO plan, decide whether it's worth it to you to pay a little more for a POS, or point-of-service, plan. This is a popular add-on with those who have a particular illness, like diabetes or glaucoma, and may want to visit a certain doctor not included under a standard HMO.

Sign Up When You're Healthy. If you're currently uninsured and break your arm, you better have money saved in the bank. In most, if not all, states, preexisting illnesses or medical conditions are not covered by HMOs for up to a year after enrolling.

Watch Out for Phonies. Health-care fraud totaled $85 billion in 2003, according to the Blue Cross Blue Shield Association and the U.S. Government Accountability Office. So, imagine what it is now, years later. A common trick: using the word *coverage* instead of *insurance* to confuse consumers into thinking they'll be covered in times of need. Do a background check by contacting your state's insurance commissioner organization.

> Compare health-care programs at www.planforyourhealth.com.

I'M IN BETWEEN JOBS. NOW WHAT?

Fight Back with COBRA. When you switch jobs (whether voluntarily or not—although if you were fired due to "gross misconduct," you're out of luck with this one), you have the right to continue being on your old health-care plan at a (more expensive) group rate. It may take a few months before your find a new job and then another couple of months before your new employer's health-sponsored insurance kicks in. In the meantime, you may be still dependent on medical care for a condition, or need certain prescription drugs covered under your previous health plan. The COBRA, or Consolidated Omnibus Budget Reconciliation Act, lets you stay on your previous health-care plan at the group rate for up to eighteen months. If you work somewhere that's exempt from this federally mandated law, don't cry just yet. A lot of states have what's called a mini-COBRA law that offers broader rights for those eligible.

Raise Your Deductible. A COBRA plan with a high-deductible option lets you pay less month to month in exchange for paying a higher deductible. If reducing your monthly cash flow is crucial, this could be a helpful solution.

RX RELAXATION—*SAVING ON DOCTOR-PRESCRIBED MEDICINE*

Prescription drugs in the United States can cost an arm and a leg. But there are ways to trim your costs, all without getting on that big Vancouver-bound bus with Grandma.

Hit the Web. Shopping online can sometimes help you save some bucks. As a precaution, make sure to only buy drugs at Verified Internet Pharmacy Practice Sites (VIPPS)—approved Internet pharmacies in the United States like www.eckerd.com, www.walgreens .com, and www.cvs.com. Both www.pillbot.com and www .pharmacychecker.com compare prices for you.

Mail-Order. If there is a prescription drug you take regularly, opt for a mail-order program that let's you buy in bulk, like as if you were buying six months' worth of toilet paper from Costco. It's way cheaper. Some good sites are www.medcohealth.com, www .caremark.com, and Express-Scripts.com.

Brand-Name, Shmand Name. The designer imposter drugs are our friends. In 2004, the average price of a generic drug was close to $29 while the average price of a brand-name prescription drug was $96, according to the National Association of Chain Drug Stores. Plus, the FDA says generics have exactly the same active ingredients and effects as brand-name drugs. So the next time you go to the doctor, say you'd prefer the generic brand. And while you're there, ask for free samples.

Double-Dose. If your doctor prescribes a 10-mg dose, ask for the 20-mg dose instead, which usually costs the same price or, in some cases, can be cheaper. It's an easy way to save 50 percent. Of course, make sure to ask your doctor if it's a pill that can be cut in half. Not all medications are made to be split.

LONG-TERM DISABILITY. GET IT.

FYI . . .

New York, California, Hawaii, New Jersey, and Rhode Island are the only states that offer their working citizens *guaranteed* short-term disability coverage. Short-term disability generally lasts up to six months and the payout averages $170/week. After that, you'll need long-term disability care.

After nearly ten years of typing twelve hours a day on a PC, my friend Lisa, a producer for a major news network, developed a nerve injury stemming from her fingers up to her elbow. Her doctor described it as a sort of carpal tunnel syndrome, only worse. Her prescription: Quit working immediately until the condition healed, i.e., indefinitely.

Luckily for Lisa, she had signed up for long-term disability (LTD) when she renewed her insurance plan earlier that year with her company. The income-replacement plan essentially allowed her to earn up to two-thirds her salary for the period she was out of work, tax free (so basically she was maintaining her paycheck). It's like life insurance, only it kicks in when you're alive. Lisa didn't realize she was covered when she was first told of her condition; she just remembered checking off some box, after realizing the so-called LTD plan would only cost her a few dollars a month. In the end, her oblivion saved her from losing an income during that six-month period.

This is essentially why long-term disability insurance is more important than life insurance in many cases, as a young, single worker. Yet too many of us are underinsured or not insured at all because of the myth that we're not likely to get physically disabled in our youth, let alone disabled for an extended period of time. But *disabled* doesn't just mean breaking a leg; it can be a technology-induced illness like my friend Lisa's nerve injury. The scope of disability has broadened in this technology age, where we rely more and more on our ability to type and sit upright to perform our jobs. In fact, according to the Social Security Department, twenty-year-old workers have a 30 percent chance of getting disabled between now and retirement.

Disability Defined. As far as insurance companies and benefits providers are concerned, there's no single definition for the term *disability*. To some it means a condition that prevents you from performing your job. To others it may mean not being able to do *any* job, like even taking burger orders at McDonald's, believe it or not.

Win Your Claim. The tricky thing about Lisa's "coverage" is that even though she had signed up for long-term disability insurance through her employer, there was no guarantee she would have been able to cash in month after month. More or less, she was lucky when her insurance company accepted her claim. That's the other annoyance, or "sicko" thing, as director Michael Moore puts it, with health insurance: It doesn't always come to the rescue, even though you've been dutifully paying your premium every month. For those convinced they'd now like to move to Canada, here are some helpful Web sites:

➤ www.canada.gc.ca: the official government Web site for Canada
➤ www.cic.gc.ca: the official immigration Web site for Canada
➤ www.crea.ca: the Canadian Real Estate Association

For those still choosing to live and work in the United States, here is some fast advice on how to win your disability claim.

Stay Informed. Experts recommend first studying the definition of *disability* in the policy. Make sure you qualify. What's more, says Steve Weisbart, an economist at the Insurance Information Institute, is, "a lot of plans will, after a period of time, say two or three years, change the term of disability." Unfortunately, change usually means it's *more* challenging for individuals to qualify, since it also (advantageously) gets insurance companies off the hook from continuing to pay you. To put it in Weisbart's words: "[Insurance companies] expect that if it's at all possible for you to make a recovery, you should do that—instead of watching soap operas all day." Oh, how I miss *Santa Barbara*.

Best to check in each year to make sure you and your healthcare company are on the same page.

Kiss Up to Your Doc. Work closely with your physician to draft the proper medical letter with evidence proving you, in fact, cannot perform your and/or *any* job of your skill level. And keep in mind: Self-reported symptoms like fatigue and pain don't fly with insurance providers because they're hard to measure. Better to give some sort of specific, medically jargoned injury or side effect, such as "distal biceps rupture" as opposed to "pain in upper arm." That should help you better cash in.

Why You Need It. If, like most of us, you have to depend on your full-time income to survive because you don't have a backup—like a second job or a big old savings account—make sure you have signed up for long-term disability insurance. It's especially important to have it if you have to support another person. Also, consider your lifestyle. If you lead a physically active life (e.g., you run marathons or participate in the annual county Roller Derby race) or have a job that requires a lot of driving, you may be more vulnerable to an unexpected injury and therefore may need long-term disability insurance.

How to Buy. Generally, if your company employs fifty or more people, it tends to sponsor some sort of long-term disability group plan that is either 100 percent or partly paid for by the employer. Popular group insurance carriers include Unum, Cigna, MetLife, and Prudential.

Check with your human resources department for more information. For those of you who don't have the option of group insurance, you can buy directly from private insurance carriers, which is more expensive. Guardian, MassMutual, and Northwestern Mutual offer various, personalized plans. You can learn more about each online.

What's It Going to Cost Me? That depends largely on the *type* of disability insurance. If it is a group plan, the most recent data from the Insurance Information Institute found the average annual premium to be roughly $218 per year, or roughly twenty bucks a month. The general rule is that if you're paying more than half a percent of your income annually, you're paying too much.

So, if you earn $35,000 a year, the insurance premium would be around $175 a year. For individual plans directly from the insurance company, the cost is significantly higher and is based on a person's age, health, and lifestyle.

How Much Can I Cash In? Generally, group policies pay up to 60–67 percent of your annual base income, not including bonuses. There may be a monthly cap as well. Furthermore, if the employee pays the entire premium, the payout is not taxed. If the employer helps to pay for the plan, the payout is taxed. Meantime, individual plans, more popular with high-net-worth individuals, tend to have no caps on payout. So, someone earning a $100,000 base salary with a $400,000 annual bonus is better off getting an individual disability insurance plan, experts say, since it may take into account the person's total earnings and it better compensates him or her in case of an emergency.

GET FLEXIBLE WITH FSAS

If you're receiving health benefits through work, chances are you're ignoring a huge tax break. Flexible spending accounts, or FSAs, are employer-sponsored pretax accounts that pay for out-of-pocket eligible medical and child-care expenses. More than 90 percent of employers offer them. Still, few people sign up for FSAs, as there's still some uncertainty about what they are and how they work.

FSAs Defined. An FSA, also called a reimbursement account, lets you set aside pretax money to pay for out-of-pocket medical expenses like health insurance premiums, deductibles, and copayments. It's tax free, so in the end it saves you money. It's completely voluntary, like a 401(k) account, and only valid for one benefit period. In other words, you have to enroll each year that you choose to participate. Check in with your company's HR office about enrolling.

How They Work. Every year, participating employers will ask how much you'd like to contribute from your pretax income into the account. There is no tax-law limit, although most companies generally allow maximum annual contributions of $6,000. Each pay period, your employer will deduct a proportionate amount. If you have an FSA debit card, you don't have to submit any forms to make your claims. All others need to download a claim form from www.fsafeds.com. Then either fax or mail your information to FSAFEDS or to your company's plan provider.

How Much to Reserve? To figure out how much to put aside, consider how much you've spent in medical expenses in the past and how much you anticipate using in the current year. Be conservative in at least the first year because whatever you don't use, you lose; don't assume you're better off maxing out. But, if you have money left over toward the end of the period, just stock up on year-round necessities like Tylenol and Band-Aids.

What's Included? The list is long and includes most over-the-counter medicines and health products, from cough syrup to dental floss. Prescription glasses are also included, as well as medical office copays. A comprehensive list is at www.fsafeds.com.

BITING YOUR DENTAL BILL

My earlier reference to getting eight cavities is no joke. My friend Amy Miller, whom I idolize in the intro to this book, seriously discovered eight cavities when she visited the dentist after college. Even with decent dental coverage, the procedures to fill eight cavities were going to fast put a hole in her pocket when you factor in her deductible for each procedure. She decided to spread out the procedures, to get a couple of cavities filled every six months to a year, in order to avoid getting one lump sum bill. That's just one way to save at the dentist. Here are some others.

Get a PPO Dentist. If your employer offers dental insurance, pick a dentist who is enrolled in the insurer's preferred provider organization, or PPO. Chances are, celebrity dentists and dentists in rich neighborhoods are not part of a plan because they have enough clients who can afford to foot the entire bill. In general, dentists who are not part of a plan charge up to 40 percent more.

PPO Isn't Possible? If your company does not offer a dental plan, you can lobby with your HR department to subscribe to a group plan that has you paying 100 percent of the premium. It's more expensive but at least gets you a group premium rate, which is cheaper than an individual dental plan.

Don't Play Dumb with Your Dentist. Don't let your dentist (who was probably a scheming car mechanic in a past life) sucker you into the most expensive treatments. Ask about cheaper alternatives. For example, a porcelain crown can run you $900. While it may not be as pretty or as durable, a simple metal filling can cost a third of that price. Again, if you are getting a lot of work done, try to spread out the appointments over two years so that you are not stuck with one giant payment that exceeds your plan's maximum annual credit. It means more visits to the dentist, but trust me, you'll be thankful when you get the dentist bill in the mail.

Barter. That's right. Everything is negotiable. My former coworker and friend Ellen McGirt, financial reporter extraordinaire, once found out that some dentists will trade services with their patients. They'll give you a cavity filling in exchange for, say, snazzying up their clinic's Web site or, if you're a lawyer, legal advice. Just be sure to let your doc know you're on a "good life" plan (notice I didn't say budget). Don't be shy!

Floss Only the Teeth You Want to Save. Just some advice my dentist always gives me. Brush your teeth at least twice and floss once a day. The American Dental Hygienists' Association found that every dollar spent on preventative care can save you up to $50 down the road in restoring your teeth.

Go Back to School. If you live near a university with a medical school, seek dental care from the school's licensed medical center run by students-in-training who act as health-care workers. I used to go to the NYU Medical Center to get my eyes checked when I was a student at Columbia for about half the price of a standard eye exam at an optometrist's office. In fact, that's where I got my first pair of contact lenses. The quality of service was just as good as at my current eye doctor.

➤ ➤ ➤ ➤ Mooch off Medical Clinics

Your county or district may have some free medical clinics for the under-insured or those without any health coverage. The Department of Health and Human Services at www.ask.hrsa.gov/pc is a great site to find a free medical clinic or camp in your area. There are also *retail* medical clinics that charge a flat fee and offer a limited number of minor checkups, from a throat check to an eye exam. Examples of retail clinics, which are rapidly growing around the country, include MinuteClinic, which is located inside various CVS/Caremark pharmacies and Targets, and InterFit, which can be found inside some Wal-Marts. Retail clinics offer walk-in service and are generally staffed by nurse practitioners. If you have a minor problem, it saves to go to one rather than to an emergency room, where the wait period can be drastically longer. The downside is you don't get as personal and professional attention as going to an MD, but if your throat is keeping you up all night, you have no insurance, and NyQuil isn't cutting it, consider stopping by a free or retail clinic to help you get out of your misery. It may cost $50 or $70, but figure it's a couple of nights out for dinner. Cook at home for the next week.

How Dustin Is Paying for His Surgery . . . sans Insurance

My buddy Dustin, who, if you remember, escaped his college loan for five years, hit a rough patch when he discovered he needed ankle surgery. He wasn't yet full-time at his job and so had no medical coverage. In short, his medical bill totaled a whopping $1,700. Dustin's surgery bills are getting paid with the help of Alliance, a credit-counseling program that's also helping him pay off his credit cards. "They don't so much consolidate your debt, but work with the individual collection agencies to reduce your interest rate," says Dustin. To learn more about Alliance visit www .knowdebt.org. The U.S Department of Justice also compiles a database of approved credit-counseling agencies. Visit www.usdoj.gov/ust/eo/ bapcpa/ccde/cc_approved.htm for the most current list.

➤ ➤ ➤ ➤ ➤ Don't Lose Your Identity at the Doc's Office

We've all heard of ID theft. It's officially the country's fastest growing crime. But it doesn't just happen because you forgot to shred your mail or you left your Social Security card in a cab. It can also happen at the doctor's office. Medical ID theft isn't a new crime, but it's one that's being closely monitored as more and more claims get filed. It's probably even worse than traditional ID theft since medical ID theft can jeopardize your health.

How it happens. Medical ID theft can occur in a few ways. The most likely scenario is when someone steals your insurance card and begins using your medical allowances. Another way is if medical personnel grab hold of your records and then hijack the information. This can be done by an employee of a medical provider, like your dentist, physician, or health insurance company.

Worst-case scenario. It's pretty bad. If you're a victim, experts caution that the history of the thief could get intertwined with your medical history, creating conditions, allergies, and blood types that aren't yours.

Prevention. More hospitals are establishing programs to prevent medical ID theft. In the meantime, ask your health provider or insurance company for an updated copy of your medical records to make sure all the information is correct—and yours.

Already a victim? Contact the antifraud unit of your insurance company first, to change your insurance ID number to prevent future losses. Next, contact the police department's white-collar crime unit. After that, get in touch with your medical provider. Occasionally the medical provider may be linked to or involved in the crime, experts say, so it's best to call them last, after you've identified the perpetrator and are positive the medical provider is not involved.

DO I REALLY NEED LIFE INSURANCE?

I never thought about it until a woman from Prudential called me at work one day to introduce me to the world of life insurance. I had no idea if I had any or needed it. My friends said I probably had some through work and they were right, but the persistent insurance agent stressed that it wouldn't be enough. The advice I got from financial experts and my parents was that basically, if you have no children or other dependents, you can pretty much *pass* on this form of insurance, since it's intended to financially serve your dependents in the event of your death. Still, if you think you'll need some, consider these steps.

Find Out How Much Coverage You'll Need. Do a "needs" analysis to figure out how much income your family or dependents will need in order to maintain their current lifestyle. Remember to factor in your expenses, all outstanding debt, a mortgage, funeral costs, and, if you have children, how much it would cost to send them to college.

Search on the Web. Begin your search by comparing quotes from hundreds of companies at Web sites like www.reliaquote .com, www.accu-quote.com, and www.insure.com. Make sure the insurance company you decide to work with has a rating of A or better from independent rating agencies like Moody's Investor Service, Standard and Poor's, or Weiss Ratings.

Ask for Recommendations. Get suggestions from family and friends.

Look into Your Employer. If your work benefits include life insurance and you feel you have enough assets, that may be all you need. But most employer-sponsored life insurance plans are limited in the amount they provide, offering just double or triple your salary. Many planners recommend a minimum of five times your salary.

VISION: 20/20 SAVINGS

I wear contact lenses and glasses, so, naturally, my expenses are relatively higher than a person with 20/20, or perfect, vision. And, boy, have I wasted money getting my eyes checked and buying contact lenses and glasses. I used to think it was all because my vision plan had weak insurance coverage, but I finally realized it was also due to the fact that my eye doctor (and my own ignorance) was robbing me blind. Here is some advice I wish I had known years ago.

If You Can't See Sharply, Speak Up! Testing your vision off those wall lettered/numbered charts is only so accurate. Granted, ophthalmologists and optometrists have very sophisticated examination tools these days, but sometimes those instruments fail to indicate the precise prescription you need. (Or, it may be your eye doctor is not smart enough to correctly interpret the results.) One of the costliest mistakes I ever made was assuming the doctor knew what she was doing. She said I didn't need a stronger prescription, just a better-fitting pair of contact lenses. Three weeks into wearing them, I started to experience headaches and blurred vision. I went back for a second trip and had to do *another* "contact lens examination," which cost me $80! My insurance wouldn't cover it because I'm only allotted one exam per year. Plus, why did I have to pay for my doctor's mistake? I walked out with a stronger prescription, yes, but $80 in the hole.

Test Out Your New Vision. If you get a pair of new glasses or lenses and they begin to hurt your vision, make sure you contact your eye doctor right away. Don't wait longer than two weeks, since many eye doctors will reimburse or reexamine you for free before the so-called trial period is over. Just make sure your eye doctor offers a free "trial period." Never assume!

Understand How Your Vision Policy Works. My vision plan covers one examination per year and either one pair of eyeglasses (frames not included) or a six-month supply of contact lenses. I get a $100 voucher toward frame wear per year, as well. But in some cases one year doesn't mean one calendar year; it may mean one year since your last visit.

Stock Up on Solution. Every time I go to the eye doctor (which is sometimes twice a year, because staring at a computer screen twelve hours a day doesn't help), I stock up on contact lens solution and maybe even pick up free frames for my glasses. Don't hesitate to ask for *schwag*!

CHAPTER 13

JUST SAY NO!
In Some Cases, Run Away!

Nancy Reagan's antidrug slogan helped keep us (well, most of us) off the smack. But the *Just Say No* mantra can do more than save us from drug dealers and death by painkillers. It can also rescue us from bad financial behavior.

My personal pet peeve: sales reps who routinely ask me for my phone number at checkout. It most recently happened to me at the new Loehmann's department store in my neighborhood (whose Theory discount rack, btw, has become a frequent hangout for yours truly). Why must they ask for my number? Is it really a mandatory part of buying discount picture frames and "irregular"-size bed sheets? The ruthless sales associate makes it seem so:

"Your phone number, please," she says, pretending I have no choice but to oblige.

"No, I'd rather not," I respond, though she is quite aggressive.

"Oh, don't worry (fake smile), we're not going to sell your number to some big marketing agency. It's just for in-house promotions."

"Well then, in that case, certainly. Please call and eat up my precious cell phone minutes to alert me of your upcoming fall leather boot sale extravaganza. I want to be the first to buy Steve Madden from eight seasons past. Also, here's my Social Security number, date of birth, and promise of firstborn son." As if I'm not in the store enough to know about upcoming sales. How insulting.

And it's not just salespeople tugging at our purse strings. It's our loved ones, friends, and coworkers, making it even harder to say no. But we mustn't be cowards! Whether it's to borrow some quick cash for lunch, money for a cab ride, or start-up funding to help launch a business, it sometimes feels like others really believe *your* money grows on trees. Just Say No (gently)! Let Cousin Joe or your college roommate down softly without compromising your relationship. Here's a how-to for some common situations.

"Hey, man, do you have some cash I can borrow? I'll totally pay you back!"

You might have an extra $25 to spare, but do you really want to give it to your old pledge brother (whom you love dearly), but who still owes you $40 from last fall's barhop? If the answer is no, then there's your reply. The bottom line is you shouldn't lend money you don't have. Just be honest and say you wish you could help, but money is really tight for you now as well. Your friend who's begging for money should obviously understand that.

On the other hand, if you have the extra money to lend (and your friend can tell because you wear $300 jeans and never look at price tags) and you want to make the loan, you have to make sure you're *comfortable* parting with the money and possibly never, *ever* seeing it again. You can't view it as a loan. It's money gone. If you suspect you'll be up all night worrying about whether you'll be paid back, all while plotting a nasty, cruel revenge on your friend, it's a sure sign that you shouldn't give the money. Remember, with small amounts of money ($25 or less), there's no borrowing contract and it isn't worth losing a friendship over. Just kiss it good-bye.

If you lend money and a certain friend or family member doesn't return the favor, let that serve as a lesson for the *next* time. But be the bigger person and realize it was *your* mistake to have ever thought that money was getting returned. It's a strange world we live in, but that's sadly how many lending situations between friends and family pan out.

Of course, for urgent situations, like when in a cab or at a restaurant and your friend forgets his or her wallet, be more realistic. (P.S. *Urgent* does not mean asking to borrow money at the mall.) Obviously, make an exception then, but don't let them off too easily. *Social Savvy* author Judith Ré suggests saying, "I'll treat you this time and you can pick up the tab next." And speak up the next time you go out. Don't be shy. Your friend wasn't shy *asking* you for money in the first place, right?

"I'm starting my own fashion line. Help!": A Lesson for Big Loans

Props to our friends for wanting to start their own businesses, to leave the nine-to-five grind and give up a dental plan as well as free office supplies all in the name of entrepreneurship. It's a risky road for them, but that doesn't imply *you* should risk your money and financial future, too. For big loans (as in those greater than $100), a simple handshake won't cut it. Whether it's for a friend's business or to help a buddy who's short on rent, *contracts are a must*.

What to Have in the Contract? State how much was borrowed, who owes what, when it needs to be paid back, and whether it will be returned in increments or all at once. Have a repayment schedule, a grace period, and the interest rate. That's right. Interest.

Considering your money could be earning up to 5 percent APR in an online savings account, make sure the interest on this loan is equal or greater. Remember to get the contract notarized and signed by a witness. It all sounds very legal-shmegal and far from friendly. But it's more common than you'd think. The friends-and-family route is one of the more popular funding channels for start-ups with more than six million friends-and-family loans per year. It's an $89 billion market, according to CircleLending, an organization whose agents create a business agreement between two parties and help service the payment loan for a fee. CircleLending's volume totaled more than $100 million in early 2006. The firm boasts an overall default rate of less than 5 percent. CircleLending recently got bought by Richard Branson's Virgin Money company. Visit www.virgin.moneyus.com for more.

➤ ➤ ➤ ➤ **Why James Lent $5,000**

While researching a story for thestreet.com on how to lend money to a friend's business, I came across thirty-two-year-old James from Indianapolis who had lent $5,000 to two childhood friends looking to open a smoothie shop in Arizona. James said he never hesitated to offer the money. "I essentially wanted to invest in my friend. I wanted to say, 'I believe in you and I know you're going to do big things,'" James says. Even his mom, Debbie, threw in $1,000. It was a smart move—Kyle and Aaron's Main Squeeze Smoothies in Buckeye, Arizona, is experiencing more than 20 percent growth year over year. James has it worked out with CircleLending that he will get his money back spread through the years with 9 percent interest. It comes down to about $86 a month into his savings account. He says he lent the money a few years back when he was a twenty-something-year-old bachelor with a well-paying software gig. "If I didn't see the money come back, it wouldn't have been devastating," he says. Life's a bit different now for James; he's since tied the knot and become a stay-at-home dad to his baby boy. His days of five-grand giveaways are over. "It wouldn't be financially feasible," says James.

➤ ➤ ➤ ➤ ➤ Should I Do It? Investing in a Friend's Business

The title of this chapter screams no, but sometimes (just sometimes) your friends might be on to something lucrative. Bear in mind, about 100,000 businesses in the United States fail each year, according to Score, a nationwide resource for small business owners. And as a reporter with a great deal of experience interviewing and writing about entrepreneurs and business owners, I can tell you, even when a business seems headed for the big leagues and it's got Nicole Kidman shopping there, it can easily go bust. Here are the two basic questions you need to ask before lending your money.

Is this person trustworthy? Whether to invest in a friend's business largely depends on how well you trust the relationship. Think twice (or eight) times before lending money to someone you just started dating. The business might do well enough for he or she to repay you (in theory), but problems with the relationship down the road may affect the repayment plan.

Is the business idea any good? And I mean, awesome. Ask for a copy of the business plan and make sure it includes sections on *how* the business plans to make money, in addition to the five-year plan. If your friend looks at you all confused when you mention the words *business plan*, take that as your cue to turn around and run away. If and when you attain the business plan, enlist an expert (like a friend at an investment bank or your parents) to evaluate whether the business is any good. But don't stop there, even if it seems like the next Pinkberry. Supplement your research by hitting the local library, which may offer free resources to look up specific sector information. Like, if your friend wants to start a coffee shop, find out how saturated the area is with coffee cafes and, of course, how many Starbucks and Dunkin' Donuts are in the region. Maybe there're already too many. How will this business stand out?

As part of your fact gathering, also make sure banks or other institutions have offered the business funding as well, be it a loan or a grant; it shows that others trust the business plan is solid. While you're at it, make sure your friend or relative is also investing a substantial chunk of his or her own money into the business. If they've got something to lose, they'll probably take the business more seriously.

Bottom line. If there's any concern that the relationship will suffer if the deal falls through the cracks, forget about it—although one thing to keep in mind is that if the investment goes bad, you *may* be able to write it off as a capital-gains loss (check with a tax preparer about that, as each case is treated differently). Remember, too, you can refer your friend to www .prosper.com, a peer-to-peer lending site.

"I'd like to tell you about an exciting opportunity that people are talking about."

Don't be dumb-fooled into pyramid scams. According to the Federal Trade Commission, pyramid schemes "concentrate on the commissions you could earn just for recruiting new distributors," and "generally ignore the marketing and selling of products and services." In other words, it's a big, awful waste of time. I speak from experience, sadly. My friend, who will remain completely anonymous so as to protect her integrity, lured me to an un-air-conditioned conference suite at the Pennsylvania Hotel in Midtown one day after work. There she and I joined about a hundred other curious idiots to listen to one helluvan enthusiastic sales pitch led by a tag team of money-hungry middle-aged men with props. Seriously, this one guy used a cowbell. In the end, I learned

I could get superrich but never found out *how* it all quite worked. I look back now and thank goodness I didn't fall into that trap, though admittedly, at the time, I kind of thought I'd discovered a fast track to wealth. I mean, really . . . do absolutely nothing and have money for a Lexus in three years? Sign me up! Excited, I called my dad and presented him with the same evangelical sales pitch over the phone. He told me I was nuts, then asked if I was broke or something. *Maybe he would have listened had I just used more cowbell. . . .*

"Would you like to save 20 percent today by opening a Banana Republic credit card?"

Okay, I have one of these—but only because I shop at BR a ton and always always pay off my balance regularly. (Well, all right, this one time I missed a payment because I misread the statement on mycheckfree.com and had to pay a $25 late fee.) So *sometimes* opening a store credit card is a decent idea. Like if you're buying a ton of stuff, then the promotional 20 percent savings can really help. Also, later down the road, using your card and paying the balance off regularly can earn you discounts. BR sends me a $10-off card for my birthday! But even then, make sure you will be a frequent shopper at the store and that you can commit to paying off the balance in full each billing period. Otherwise, store credit cards offer zero incentives and could end up costing you money, actually. Why? Because you know how every time you sign up for a store credit card, the sales rep asks if you can just wait five minutes while she "verifies your information"? Well, in that brief period of time, while you patiently wait and consider buying more crap from the small sale bin at the register (ooh! fork and spoon–shaped earrings!), you are getting poorer. The person on the other end of the phone is running an "inquiry" on your credit report, which is bad news for your credit score and could mean higher rates on other things—such as a car loan—down the road.

And what's worse, a store credit card usually has a very low credit line, like $500 or $750, and so a few purchases can quickly raise that key debt-to-available-credit ratio we went through earlier on in the book that weighs big time on your credit score. You want to keep your debt-to-credit ratio at or below 30 percent.

"Would you like to buy an extended warranty?"

A store's warranty is usually money down the drain, considering most consumers never use it. In fact, stats show retailers rake in up to 40 percent of their gross revenue from extended warranties, which basically means buyers don't act on them. Plus, the store could always go out of business, which essentially flushes your warranty down the drain.

Really, all you need when buying an item with a serious price tag is the manufacturer's own warranty, which is almost always available at no extra cost. This warranty lets you exchange the item if it breaks during a certain period from the date of purchase.

"Wanna rent a summer house with eight of our friends?"

Are you crazy? A big mistake, yet something almost every overly excited hot-out-of college grad considers the first time they're in the real world. Unless you enjoy sharing one rusting bathroom with eight people in a rickety shack in the Hamptons, where beer pong and flip cup go 'round the clock, don't do this. Please! A few summers ago, my friend Tracy forked over $1,200 to share a thirty-five-person "beach house" in Bridgehampton. She never went back. "It was with a huge group of people I didn't know and frankly, didn't much like." Plus, without a car, Tracy felt stranded at the beach house, which was actually miles away from the shore. Now she vacations by the Jersey Shore, where she grew up and where the crowd isn't as high maintenance. "The whole Hamptons scene was a little too New York City. I felt underdressed if not in a Juicy Couture tracksuit and heels around the pool."

➤ ➤ ➤ ➤ ➤ **Before You Share . . .**

Consider these tips before putting down money for a summer share with friends.

If it sounds too good to be true . . . You know the rest. Whatever your expectation is, lower it. Don't be easily persuaded by ads that boast "housekeeping" and "a walk's distance from the beach." Don't feel pressured by your peers to join a deal just because your buddies think it's a genius plan.

The roommates: Know them—all of them. The biggest mistake, experts say, is not meeting enough people in the house beforehand. That may seem impossible if the house fits dozens of people, but usually the organizer or house manager will plan a happy hour or gathering for potential renters. If not, ask that they do. You risk ending up in a house that's annoying and obnoxious.

The house: Go there ahead of time. Don't just trust a photo of the house's exterior. Examine the interior by visiting the actual home. It may be a hassle to get there, but it's worth spending an afternoon to inspect a place in which you'll likely spend several weekends. If you can't visit, call up someone who has stayed there in the past. And at least map the property online to verify its proximity to town and the beach—a must for those who may not have access to a car. Otherwise, expect to pay a lot of money for cabs.

The cost: Prepare to pay at least $1,000. For a house share, renters can usually sign up for either a whole, half, or quarter of the season. That translates into sixteen, eight, or four weekends, respectively. For a quarter share, experts say, expect to pay an average of $1,200 to $1,350, but no more than $1,400. For a half share, anything more than $2,500 is a rip-off.

"Want to go to the Calvin Klein sample sale?"

Why? So I can spend my money on stuff no one wanted even when it was *in* season? So I can risk getting my face scratched in a feisty crowd of four hundred time-pressured, high-heeled New York women, as we scour through cardboard boxes and racks of still-too-expensive clothing we wouldn't have even looked at when it was full priced at Barneys? Don't be suckered into thinking a sample sale will necessarily have the best deals in town. You're better off hitting the discount rack at Bloomingdale's, where you can also *return* the item if you're not pleased. Sample sales usually just accept cash or check and returns are hardly ever, if at all, allowed. The only exception to when it is permissible to shop at a sample sale is if the brand is one you'd *truly* wear, I mean cherish and worship. Like, you would wear the outfit to bed. Bottom line: It's gotta be part of your good-life equation. And, well, you know me and DVF. One winter, a coworker and I took a $16 cab ride from work to get first dibs on a Diane von Furstenberg sample sale. She knew the store manager so we were able to preview the sale with the so-called DVF "friends and family" before all the "commoners" would flood in to fight over the last wool, pleated, hot pink miniskirt. I was first in line for mine. I bought a wrap dress for $50 (originally close to $400) and another for $100 (also, originally close to $400). I wear them *all* the time. I wore one to my job interview at thestreet.com. Her clothes make me feel confident, and that is so money!

CHAPTER 14

MONEY IS EVERYWHERE

For Serious!

There are opportunities everywhere to make money, and we, as a young, energetic, and bright crowd, have the highest potential to capitalize on this than any other demographic. For one, we have the stamina. While I can no longer stay up until 4 A.M. and roll into work, I can probably keep awake until midnight or 1 A.M. My college body clock is somewhat still intact. This has allowed me to, for example, write a book and freelance write for various publications.

And on weeknights, occasionally, I will babysit little Luke and Blake, the two most precious baby boys in all of Manhattan. Their parents pay me a very generous $15 to $20 an hour, plus money for ordering in dinner and taking a cab home. On average, I make about $75 a night. That's not including my free meal and lessons in parenting. And while the boys are asleep, I can catch up on my writing assignments or watch the latest episode of *Entourage* on-demand. It's pretty perfect.

That $75 will later go to pay for my Saturday night (or, *most* of my Saturday night, depending). I see my babysitting earnings as guilt-free spending money. If I was more fiscally responsible, I suppose I'd take that money and put it into a savings or retirement account, but that's no fun. And remember, if this book will leave you with any lessons, it's that you can have fun and still be fiscally responsible. After all, what's the point of earning money if you never get to enjoy it?

My example of making money outside of my nine-to-five is far from savvy, when you consider what my coworkers and friends have been up to in their young-adult years. Also, it's chump change when you consider how much money my friend Kat, a television producer by day, makes after just a Saturday afternoon babysitting three siblings in the Hamptons (ahem, $400).

From creating profitable Web sites to launching a beauty company and directing an off-Broadway play, the profiles you are about to read prove there are no limits to fulfilling your career dreams, even when you have a full-time job. It can be discouraging at times to work someplace where we feel underutilized or where the corporate ladder is skewed by politics. Instead, create your own career. It is one ultimate way to control your financial future.

WILL BLOG FOR MONEY

Moneymaker: Michelle
Age: early thirties
Likes: red wine and shopping online
A prized purchase: her own one-bedroom apartment in Manhattan
  before turning thirty
Schooling: Northwestern

In 2004, Michelle left a six-figure salary at America Online to start a full-time blog, all at a time when "blogs" were considered hokey and useless. By its third year, her shopping blog, shefinds .com, was raking in half a million dollars a year.

How She Financed It? She spent only $250 to develop the Web site and runs it out of her New York City apartment. She has about twenty freelance writers across the country who contribute editorial content, many of them budding scribes getting more value from the experience than from the paycheck (i.e., cheap labor).

How Does It Make Money? The blog makes money by selling banner ads, but the bulk of revenue stems from the site's retail placements. Product reviews and articles always include where consumers can find mentioned items. If readers actually go on to buy the items, shefinds.com earns a commission, as much as 15 percent. Shefinds.com's target audience is made of fashion-conscious working women with disposable income and little time to search for the latest must-haves. "It's not about impressions," says Michelle. "It's about who you impress." Shefinds.com is now working with www.amazon.com and AOL. It also has advertising and sponsorship deals, as well as commission-based relationships, with roughly one hundred various online retailers, including www.nordstrom.com, the shoe site www.zappos.com, www.eluxury.com, www.barenecessities.com, and www.neimanmarcus.com.

Networking, she added, is helping the site win major business and more annual income. Michelle makes herself meet four people a week who can help her grow her business and makes sure to follow up.

➤ ➤ ➤ ➤ ➤ **More on Making Bucks with Your Blog**

Google it. Google's free AdSense service is how many Web sites make money—blogs included. Based on your blog's content and target audience, Google displays context-related ads along the top and side of the site. For example, if your blog is about fashion, ads for clothing retailers may appear on the site. Google doesn't disclose the exact percent of revenue you'll receive other than to say that when a reader clicks the ad, you make some money. Search www.google.com/adsense for more.

"Ad" it up. In addition to Google's help, you can draw advertisers on your own and set your own rates. To make your site attractive, market your blog's distinctive audience and niche content. Prove to would-be advertisers that you've got a constant flow of targeted readers by ramping up traffic. To get help tracking your site's page views, try Web site services like www.statcounter.com, www.gvisit.com, and www .sitemeter.com.

Get paid per post. If you're not a blog owner but enjoy blogging all over the blogosphere, many online businesses pay bloggers to write about products, Web sites, and companies. Visit www.payperpost.com and www.weblogs.com to start working.

Click through and cash in. Make agreements with other sites so that if your blog or Web site facilitates traffic by referring readers there, you can make some money.

Juice it up. Again, this is a Google thing. Giving Google *juice* is when you give the search engine search words that are related to the site but not limited to its name or main content. A site with a lot of juice ranks high among Google search results.

GETTING DRAMATIC

Moneymaker: Alix
Age: twenty-nine
Likes: yoga and healthy living
Guilty pleasures: Sour Patch Kids and YouTube
Schooling: Northwestern

After her job as a production coordinator at thestreet.com TV ends at 6 P.M., my coworker Alix goes to her "passion job." A Northwestern graduate, she studied theater and then raced back to New York, where she was born and raised, to get her career on track. She picked up "money jobs," as she calls them, to support her ambitions of directing theater or working in a production company full-time. "I have been lucky enough over the past year and a half to get some theater gigs. I started taking classes at an off-Broadway theater company and everything fell into place. It has a professional production company, as well. I prop-designed two shows and directed three."

Her highest-paying gig? $400. Her lowest: $100. "I by no means count on this money. It usually goes into my savings for two and a half seconds, until I do something like buy a rug or go grocery shopping or take more cabs than I should," she says. "Also, I can be happy that I can go out to eat and not worry about the bill."

How does Alix stay awake? Zinc vitamins. "I have also started drinking coffee again (decaf, but still it helps)." She tries to get an average of six hours of "passion work" a week.

BEAUTY MATTERS

Moneymaker: Rashida
Age: twenty-seven
Schooling: University of Rochester
Likes: Broadway shows and *People* magazine

When I met Rashida at a summer internship program, I knew instantly that she was destined for great things. The first week we hung out, she pitched me a business idea and wanted to know if I'd be her partner. Sadly, we were twenty-one and broke, but Rashida didn't let down.

Today, she's the owner of Marie Deneen cosmetics, a beauty brand she started in her apartment, all while working full-time as an art and photo designer for magazines. It hasn't started earning enough money for her to quit her day job, but that's her hope. For now, on top of the beauty line and her full-time job, Rashida works as a freelance graphics artist, earning about $900 every two to three months. That money goes straight into her savings account, she says. Well, sometimes it pays for her Broadway tickets and dinner with friends. She's human, after all.

DOODLING FOR DOLLARS

Moneymaker: Dee
Age: twenty-nine
Born: Abilene, Texas
Loves: creating films, cartoons, and music

Dee works full time for a media company in Manhattan, but has his hands in both the East and West coasts doing various side media projects. For extra dough, he produces films and videos for various companies, and since he can shoot, edit, and distribute the media himself, his overhead costs are kept at a minimum.

Where does his extra money go? To pay off his school loans, credit-card debt, and funding his own creative short films and videos.

Long-term goal: To be debt-free and direct feature films.

BUILD A WEB SITE AND THEY WILL COME

Moneymaker: Matt
Age: twenty-five
Schooling: James Madison University

Likes: Roller Derby and free beer
Career goal: "I just want to be my own boss so I can wake up at noon
and work all day in my underwear."

Matt is a video producer by day and moonlights as a freelancer doing basically any media-related job that earns him good money—including jobs for advertising agencies doing video, Flash, multimedia, HTML, PowerPoint, or other computer-related assignments.

How does he find work? "People call me with work they have available and I try not to say no, because they will always remember me saying no. If I have a lot of spare time available or need some extra money for vacation or something, I'll call around to see if anyone has any work they need done, or troll Craigslist and other sites to see if anything is listed."

Where Matt's extra money goes: To pay his taxes and buying a moped, alcohol, and "various other things most people would consider wasteful."

Matt's other moneymaker: www.sageurbanite.com. This is the site I mentioned earlier that he started in 2006 out of his one-bedroom apartment in Brooklyn. It's yet to earn any substantial income, but it's highly trafficked. Matt works on the site at least four days a week, which admittedly puts him on an awful sleep schedule. Some mornings he wakes up at five, works on it for three hours, works on his day job until 6:30 P.M., then works on the site again at home until midnight. At that point, he'll usually collapse. "Other times I don't look at it for a couple days; otherwise I wind up getting sick of it. It's a matter of balancing social life, work life, and enterprising life."

Make Money on Vacation

In 2006, I got three weeks of vacation. I used most of it to see my family in San Francisco and the rest to visit friends locally or just bum around my neighborhood. No matter where I was, I usually kept working. While, yes, being on vacation should mean relaxing, it can also benefit a second career. Call me crazy. My mom is still mad at me for burying myself in my laptop for hours on end while out west. But it was actually nice working in my PJs and in a living room, as opposed to sitting in my cubicle wearing three-inch heels. I felt more creative and relaxed. I reported an article most of the week I was in San Francisco and joined conference calls to pitch this book to several publishers. I also used a few days of my vacay to write the book, because I found it was hard to get revved up to write after a ten-hour day. The momentum needs to start building earlier in the day. Matt and Dee agree. They, too, will take off from work to dedicate time to their side projects.

➤ ➤ ➤ ➤ Not So Fast . . . the Freelance Tax

All of your "supplementary" income is taxable unless specifically excluded by law, according to the Internal Revenue Service. That means even if there's no paper trail tracking the money earned from your babysitting gigs or freelance work, you're required by law to report it. In general, under the current tax law, if your annual net earnings from self-employment total $400 or more, you must file a return. The tax form to keep an eye out for is the Schedule C or Schedule C-EZ, which is what the self-employed or small business owners use to file their income and business expenses.

➤ ➤ ➤ ➤ Deduct It!

While the IRS expects you to fess up over your freelance income, there is a way to reduce your overall taxable income by deducting any and all costs related to running your side "business." This includes meals, entertainment expenses, your cell phone, your new laptop, the cost of using your car (gas, tune-ups, tire changes, etc.). If you do your freelance work out of your home, you can even deduct some of your rent or mortgage, including how much you've paid to maintain the home (e.g., gas, renovations, common charges, etc.). Make sure to take a picture of your office, in case the IRS gets curious. Never throw away any receipts related to your business and keep all your files in a safe, waterproof and fireproof spot.

THE PART-TIME PAY RAISE

Pump up your earnings with a part-time job.

Tutoring. Whether it's to help a kid brush up on algebra or teach the high school crowd how to ace the SATs, there are lots of part-time opportunities to tutor. The working hours are likely to accommodate your schedule, too, since it has to be done after school and on the weekends. Some ways to find a job include enlisting your services on Craigslist, checking campus bulletin boards, and getting in touch with tutoring companies like Kaplan (www.kaplan .com), Princeton Review (www.princetonreview.com), Sylvan (www .tutoring.sylvanlearning.com), and Score! (www.escore.com).

Food Service. Someone's gotta work the graveyard shift at the local twenty-four-hour diner! If you're a night owl and don't mind dealing with the 2 A.M. drunk crowd, like my friend Dustin, who occasionally works the overnight shift at Jerry's Famous Deli in L.A., this could be a great part-time fit.

Another job in this sector includes working at the local farmer's market or food coop on the weekends. My friend Mia was a member of the Park Slope, Brooklyn, food co-op, which didn't earn her bucks but did earn her steep discounts on groceries. Her membership required a $25 nonrefundable joining fee and a $100 contribution to the co-op, which she can get back once she ends her membership.

Retail. My J-school friend Susie worked at Banana Republic in the evenings for a summer while working at a nonprofit organization (read: making no money) during the day. Many clothing stores have flexible shifts, since many who work there probably have second or third jobs. Next, know that retailers, particularly department stores, get desperate for workers around the holiday season, hiring hundreds of thousands of temporary workers to help stock shelves, ring up sales, and assist returns. As an example, my friend Amanda worked evenings at Macy's one December for three weeks straight around Christmas and New Year's. She earned enough to pay off all her holiday shopping expenditures ($3,000). Plus, as an employee she had access to mad discounts and saved 40 percent on a Dooney & Bourke purse for her mom! To find jobs, visit your local mall or shopping strip no later than October to see if stores are hiring a temporary staff for the holiday period.

➤ ➤ ➤ ➤ More Easy Money Opps

Got no interest in starting your own side business? That's cool. Still want to make extra money? You got it. These sporadic side gigs have helped out me and my friends from time to time, especially while lusting for a fancy smart phone.

Freelance Write. Freelance writing is probably easiest for those working in the editorial world already, but if you want to make money off a cool story or idea, ask friends in the industry for the hookups! Ask around for the names and e-mails of editors at the various related news outlets and send them strong pitches along with your resume and clips. (Note: Make sure you tell your full-time employer about your freelance jobs—in case there's a strict policy against it.) At big magazines you may earn $2 per word, but only if you're an established writer. If you're a novice, you may earn more like $1.00 to $1.50 per word at big papers; local publications may pay as little as 25¢ to 50¢ per word. The forums at www.mediabistro.com have helpful discussions about what various media outlets pay.

Babysit. If you loathe children, this isn't for you. But if you can tolerate a night of Thomas the Tank Engine, a diaper change, and the endless question "Why?" try babysitting for some extra *dinero*. Just call up friends or friends of friends who are expecting or have young children and offer your services. You'll probably make a lot more than your babysitting days in high school. Sitters out of college usually earn more money because of their age and experience; based on my anecdotes, the average rate these days is about $10 to $12 an hour for one child. That's pretty average for a college grad. It could be more if the sitter is asked to spend the night. That may or may not include extras like a cab ride to and from home or money for dinner. My friend Catherine, twenty-nine, babysits three siblings on the Upper East Side, with the youngest usually in bed before she arrives. Her rate averages $20 to $25 per hour. "Also, the kids are wonderfully behaved, so perhaps I'd desire more [money] if they were little hellions," she says. "One of the great things about babysitting is that not only do you make money, it keeps you from spending it by giving you an alternate plan to going out."

Sell on eBay. Your Adam Sandler DVD collection and old books from AP English may generate fast cash on eBay. More than

700,000 Americans earn part or all of their income by selling on the online auction Web site. Here are some tips:

➤ **What sells:** When was the last time you bought an outfit off eBay? Probably a long time, if ever. Results show DVDs, books, and consumer electronics get sold more frequently, than say, clothes (unless it was once worn by, say, Lady Di). I couldn't even sell a never-before-worn cocktail dress for 99¢! P.S. The most surefire item to sell on eBay? Cars! That's right, eBay Motors brings in more revenue than any other category of items and has sold more than 2 million cars.

➤ **Barriers to a sale:** Make your sale listing buyer-friendly. Avoid restrictive payment options, high shipping costs, and "no return" policies. Consider selling internationally, too.

➤ **Suiting up:** Photos are a must, and the more angles the better. Also, make the item's description easy to read. Experts say bullet points are very effective. Fancy fonts are not. Fancy fonts are like bad perfume—distracting and unpleasant.

➤ **Best time to sell:** People tend to search for collectibles and hobby items on weekends, when they have more time to peruse the interweb. Office and business products usually do best during work hours.

➤ **Price to profit:** EBay experts recommend starting with a low price, about a third of what you expect to sell it for, to generate buzz and bidding wars. For example, if you think you can sell your 1987 Atari console for $100, start the bidding at around $30, or a third of the price you expect to sell.

Review Products for Blogs. At www.reviewme.com, the site pays people to blog reviews about products and other Web sites and companies. The rate may vary between $20 and $200 for each review, according to its Web site. Other sites like www.spon soredreviews.com and www.payperpost.com offer similar deals.

Sell at Consignment Shops. Rather than donating some of your old junk to charity (which is always nice—and tax deductible), hit up the local consignment or secondhand store and see if you're "vintage" pair of Stuart Weitzman pumps can secure a spot in the display window. How consignment shops work is, they agree to add your item to the store's stock of items, if they think it can sell. If it does, you get a percentage of the sale. I use the Stuart Weitzman example because once I saw a gorgeous pair of SW black satin pumps from the 1960s on display at a consignment store in Springfield, Pennsylvania. After throwing my body against the display window, I went inside praying they'd fit my size 7 1/2 feet. Miraculously, they slipped on perfectly. I paid $40—a steal for me and some extra ka-ching for the original owner (who has fabulous taste, I might add).

Pick Up "Event" Jobs. Annual or biannual events like fashion week, film festivals, and the U.S. Open are always seeking part-time help. While covering the Luella Bartley fashion show in New York on a Sunday afternoon, I ran into my book club friend Jillian, who was working as a production assistant at the show. Jillian, by day, is an editor for a publishing house, so it confused me to see her there. But, as she explained, she works at the various fashion shows when she can to make some extra cash. How she got the gig? Her coworker knows someone who knows someone who works for the show's main sponsor. Check out each event's Web site for job inquiries.

My Top Ten Titles That Didn't Make the Final Cut

1. *Kiss My Assets*
2. *Rich People Dress Good*
3. *Get More (of Everything)*
4. *Me No Want Be Poor*
5. *Poverty Shmoverty*
6. *Poor Is So Last Season*
7. *Afford Your Life*
8. *Cheer up, Po' Folk!*
9. *Filthy Stinkin' Rich: A User's Guide*
10. *The DaVinci Code*

In the end, Vince Vaughn's character said it best in the 1996 film *Swingers*: "You're so money" (although, potential title number 4 still makes my stomach hurt from laughing). But my title needed attitude since managing your money well is all about having the right state of mind. I hope you laughed at my silly money stories and found the humor in how we woefully manage our finances. I hope you reached a point where you can see through the thick cloud of debt, and along the way became intrigued by real estate or stocks. My hope with this book is not that you'll finish thinking, "Golly wow, how 'bout that compound interest!" Instead, I hope you'll feel braver, more confident, and more compelled to seize your finances and work toward achieving your "good life."

Index

About the Author

Farnoosh Torabi is a television, print, and Web journalist whose business reports and interviews air on thestreet.com TV. She joined in July 2006 as the site's first official video correspondent. Previously, Farnoosh was a business producer and on-air reporter for NY1 News, Time Warner's twenty-four-hour news channel in New York City. Farnoosh is a regular business columnist for *AM New York* and has written for *Money, Time,* the *New York Daily News* and *Newsday*. She is a graduate of Pennsylvania State University, with a degree in finance and international business and holds an M.A. from the Columbia School of Journalism.